*God ble[ss]
and Ed
stories (short but true)!
Your friend,
Ruth (Beckdahl) MacKinney*

Angels Ride Shotgun

Ruth (Merian) Beckdahl MacKinney

Angels Ride Shotgun
Ruth (Merian) Beckdahl MacKinney
Copyright 2004

Library of Congress Number 2003111504

ISBN 1-930052-12-X

Cherokee Books
P.O. Box 463
Little Creek, DE 19961

Introduction

This is "part" of my mother's story. It is a multicultural adventure made up of vignettes unique to another time and less familiar places. It is a story of a family that came from many lands to North America and became citizens of the United States. It goes without saying that we are affected by our origins. These things really happened.

I wish you could know my mother as I do. Her life has had as many twists and turns as anyone I have ever known. She is a gracious lady who has adapted admirably over and over again. She is an adventurer, an artist, a compassionate teacher, a philosopher, a wonderful conversationalist, and a dear friend. She is generous with all she has ever had and most especially in sharing herself with others.

In recent years, people like her have been called, "third culture persons," meaning that they have one foot in one culture and the other foot in another but do not really belong to either. Missionary kids often fall into this group. While this can be a complicated position to hold, it can also be fabulously rewarding. Complex societies relate differently in other places. Our values may not be the same as theirs and visa versa. Understanding this and relating well in these situations takes great care and flexibility and grace. I am thankful for both my parents. They have been examples of adaptability and good will.

What we become in the end is due to many influences. I am so grateful for Mom's taking the time to write these things down. My life has certainly been affected by the paths she has walked. Those whom we have followed have also added to our lives even though we may not have known them personally. Heritage is a great thing. I want to be part of passing it on.....Thank you, Mom, for the wonderful experiences I had as a child and the foundations of faith and practice you helped build in my life.

Esther Elise (Beckdahl, Hughes) Eley

Foreword

Introductions shouldn't be long and this one won't be! However, an explanation would be helpful. This is not a chronological story exactly but rather a bunch of poignant memories as they came to mind. I finally wrote some of them down. Family and friends have continued to ask me over the years to do this. So, here they are: some are funny, some sad, some taught me lessons, all are true. Undoubtedly, they could have been written better. I was always going to do a better job, "when I had the time." I am now eighty years old. That time factor is fast diminishing.

This is written mostly for my family to whom I want to leave the message that serving a living, loving God is the only way to live. Whether as a missionary overseas, or in your own back yard, we are all "called ones", if we belong to Him. And I want to tell my friends who read these words that God is faithful to His children. He can be trusted to keep His Word, no matter what happens in life. Reading and believing His Word daily is a privilege and a must!

This book is dedicated to my friends Ardith Brown and Celia Sutherland, my co-workers of many years ago in the Customer Service Department of the Gospel Publishing House, in Springfield, Missouri. They made me promise I'd write down some of these stories which I'd relate during our coffee breaks

My enduring thanks to my beloved daughters,

Esther and Beth who kept after me to write and didn't give up on me. Their constant, "You can do it, Mom," spurred me on. Thanks Beth, for moral backbone when I didn't think I could. Thank you, Esther, for all your encouragement and hard work, transposing my handwritten book to computer, proofreading and getting the manuscript ready and not letting me quit. God bless you both.

I love you dearly,
Mom
Ruth (Merian) Beckdahl MacKinney

Table of Contents

Introduction 3
Foreword 5
Chapter 1   Roots 9
Chapter 2   A Piece of Linen Thread 14
Chapter 3   The Saga of Mrs. Sugar 16
Chapter 4   The Most Embarrassing
               Moment of My Entire Life 20
Chapter 5   "Hi, You on the Other Elephant"
               (How Sam and I Met) 25
Chapter 6   Beginnings 29
Chapter 7   Ali Baba and the Forty Thieves 35
Chapter 8   "And Balaam's Donkey Spoke..." 65
Chapter 9   Accident on Monkey Boulevard 68
Chapter 10 Bath Time With the Crocks 72
Chapter 11 Tiger Tracks 74
Chapter 12 Angels Ride Shotgun 76
Chapter 13 The Odyssey Continues 82
Chapter 14 "And Solomon Awoke, and
               Lo It Was a Dream *I Kings 3:15* 98
Chapter 15 "Dr. Jesus will See You Now" 102
Chapter 16 "Uhuru" 107
Chapter 17 Bonnie and Clyde (Stateside) 112

MY FAMILY

Chapter 18 Daniel Frederick — "Oh, Danny Boy..." 118
Chapter 19 Esther Elise — Every Child Should
               Have a "Gramma" Like Esther 135

Chapter 20 Elizabeth Anne "Artist Extrodinaire!" .153
Chapter 21 Joseph Christian....
"Up, Up, and Away" (Joe's Story) 171
Chapter 22 Samuel Thelle Beckdahl
"Home Is Where God Takes Us" 186
Chapter 23 Verne Ballard MacKinney —
"Verne, The Icing on My Cake" 196

— Chapter 1 —

Roots

It all started with Grandpa and Grandma Merian when they left Switzerland for the "Promised Land" or the young country of the United States of America. They, with their three sons, Ernest, Walter, and James, and with another child, "on the way," reached Ellis Island in New York harbor.

Grandpa was a good worker and found employment quickly and established the family in an apartment in New Jersey. Soon after their arrival, Freddie was born. He was known to the family affectionately as "Fritz." My Dad was very young, about three and a half years old when the family moved to New York City. Before long Ella was born, followed by Lillian. Everyone who saw Ella declared that she was an "angel child." The whole family thought so, too. Not only was she beautiful, but she had a sweet, angelic nature and showed it. The family all concurred that when she suddenly died and "went to Heaven," she was too perfect to live as a human so God took her to live with Him. After her death, Naomi was born. This was their whole family

Grandpa August was everything to Grandma Elise. He was a "good man" and a good provider. He never opened his pay envelope but always laid it in Grandma's hands with a kiss. She was a wise spender and the planner for the family. Grandpa also left "spirituality" to Grandma, because he felt she was stronger in her faith and practices. Being a Salvation Army Captain, Grandma raised the children strictly in the fear and admonition of the Lord. As a very young boy, my dad started accompanying his mother to "knee drill," the Prayer Fellowship meetings. It didn't matter if it was the summer or the coldest part of the winter in the snow, these were held on the sidewalks of New York City. They were recognized by the family as partners in things "spiritual."

Grandma Elise wanted to be a foreign missionary and kept asking God to allow her to be one. The Lord did not grant Grandma her request for foreign service but never was there a lady who did more to exemplify a missionary dedication. She constantly took food to shut-ins, opened her purse to those who were in need, took in transients, where she dispensed Scripture with food and a place to sleep. So, no, God did not send Grandma overseas as a missionary but He sent her children in that roll! Ernest was called by God to China for seventeen years. Fred followed God's call to North India for forty years. Lillian went to South Africa as a missionary. Naomi went as a missionary to New York City where her life and dedication to His service was uppermost in all her dealings with anyone who needed her in that great "mission field." Grandma's grandchildren were born in America, China, India, Japan, and South Africa!

Now here is where I, Ruth Elise, one of her many grandchildren, start my story:

I was the second child born to Fred and Lillian who answered God's call to North India, specifically, on the border of Nepal. My older sister Hope was born a few months after Mom and Dad landed in Bombay and went up country by train to Saharanpur, the place where they were sent to learn the language. Dad studied Hindi while Mom worked on Urdu, the language of the Muslims. Twenty one months later they were in Lakhimpur, Kheri District, in a small mud house with bars for windows. Dad was building the mission bungalow about three miles away. While he was away procuring metal, bricks and tiles for the roof, my mother suddenly realized she was in labor although this was two months early. Time and babies wait for no one.

My mother was alone except for Hope in the "crib," to deliver herself of her second baby, me. Being a nurse, she knew what to do. There was one problem though. She saw a very poisonous tiny snake under the bed! At the moment there was nothing she could do about that except pray, which she did, and the Karite slithered away. One of the drawers in the small bureau became my cradle. Several days later a civil surgeon of the area pronounced me, "four pounds of baby."

I was two and a half by the time the mission house was ready for use. All building and grounds were constructed by hand and very few tools. The building was large and solid and had gone up with much prayer. The brick walls were thick and the roof was covered with heavy red clay tiles. Inside, the walls were whitewashed where the salamanders skittered across, eating mosquitoes and bugs. The floors were laid with large cement slabs. There were large verandahs all around the outside for shade. It was the home I longed for when I grew and had to go away to boarding school in the mountains

We enjoyed playing with the Indian children. Many times our parents asked us the meaning of some of the Indian words. We would laugh because we thought it funny that they wouldn't know something that we did! I learned later that they got the language the hard way while we merely absorbed it. It was painless for us to converse in Hindi or Urdu or Hindustani (a mixture of both). When we went to the mountains to school we had to speak English. That was no problem either as that is what our parents spoke.

Soon we had two younger brothers, first Bob and then Walter. We always had pets, usually mastiff dogs from Tibet and a cat or two. Once an orphaned deer made its home with us.

We came home from boarding school in the winter because the mountains were too cold then. Summer time in the plains was too hot so the school year took its break during winter when the whole family packed up and lived in a tent and camped on or near a river on the border of Nepal. We were not allowed into Nepal but the Nepalese came across the border to sell baskets of tangerines. They were simply delicious. Dad would gather the men together and share the good Gospel News with them and give them lots of tracts and Scripture portions to take back in their baskets. My mother always had a dispensary where we "helped" her. We would encourage women to bring their ailing babies and children and their own unbelievable ailments. How often we watched as she held their sick children in her arms and put salve on their boils and told them how to make healing caron oil with lime and linseed oil. She prayed for each patient. They held on to her hands long after the medicine and prayers were over

An incident leaps to mind right after my little brother Walter was born in the mountain cottage in Landour. He was placed in a laundry basket on a table near the empty fireplace. Mom always kept a large stainless steel thermos bottle of hot water on the mantle above his basket. That afternoon when mother, brother, and sister went to the dining room I asked to stay near my new little brother. Suddenly there was a violent earthquake and I saw the big thermos topple and come down straight over Walt's head. I could only watch in horror, it happened so fast. Even as I gazed I saw it stop in mid-air over him and remain there! I was too short to try to grab it and too scared to take my eyes off it.

    I ran to get my mother who was herding the other children out the door. I couldn't explain to her what I had just witnessed, nor did I have to. I merely grabbed her hand and pulled her towards the baby. There she saw what I couldn't explain and she burst out in praise as she grabbed both ends of the heavy thermos bottle suspended over Walter, by no visible means, She explained later that God had sent His angels to hold it so it wouldn't crash into Walter's head.

    From that time on I became aware of angels. Through the years God often sent angels to minister to me. Sometimes I saw them. Sometimes I just saw what they did or saved me from. I have written some of these incidents in this little book. They are written to let all God's children realize the wonderful provision our loving God has made for us who believe His promises.

— *Chapter 2*—

A Piece of Linen Thread

Being in boarding school was sometimes fun, and sometimes not fun! As a small child of six or seven I accepted the fact that everyone had to go to boarding school while our parents were down on the plains doing the Lord's work.

One of the fun things we looked forward to as boarders was the story hour before bedtime when our matron would read us a chapter or two of a "to be continued" story. We would brush our teeth, climb into our pajamas, slippers and robes and sit or lay on our beds with our chins propped in our hands and listen intently

One such evening my world collapsed. I sat on the side of my bed and while listening to the story, leaned down to pick up a piece of red thread from the floor mat. The girl in the bed next to mine suddenly jumped up and announced to the matron and the dorm that she had lost a rupee. This was a large silver coin about the equivalency of a quarter. To most of us girls that was an enormous amount of money. While she was the daughter of wealthy British train officials, most of us never saw a fourth of that much pocket money!

Miss Gasper, the matron, suggested we all look around our beds to see if we could retrieve the lost coin. No one spotted it anywhere. One girl in our line of beds said that she had seen me pick it up between the beds a little earlier.

No amount of denying the charge made me "Not

Guilty." Even the matron lectured me on the evils of theft and then lying on top of that! My heart was broken and I was shamed in front of all my friends. The matron declared I would have to pay weekly from my pocket money until the other girl was completely repaid. That would take eight weeks! Moreover, I could not sit on my bed at story time but had to sit on her steps, a rise of four steps to the level of her room, while the stories were being read

I was devastated! I felt humiliated! I hated school! I wanted my Mother or my Father! They would believe me!

I carried that scar for many years. But later when reading the story of Joseph in the Bible I realized God saw the truth and He would vindicate me. What others or the devil wanted to do to me as evil, God meant it for my good. The good that came from that experience was that I became aware of the hurt and harm done when a child is accused *falsely* for some action. To this day I am grateful for that lesson learned. My eventual role as an elementary school teacher gave me many opportunities to make judgments.

I am glad to say I didn't get my mental exercise by "jumping to conclusions." I made so many friends through my teaching years. I recently came across a certificate made out to me. I had been voted by the senior high school class as their all time favorite teacher! What a rewarding and affirming gift that has been to me!

Matthew 7:1 "Do not judge or you too will be judged.

For in the same way you judge others, you will be judged."

— Chapter 3—

The Saga of Mrs. Sugar

Sweet by name and sweet by nature, "Auntie" Amy Sugar was a lovely lady. As we grew up on the mission field, all lady missionaries were our "Aunts," and the men were all "Uncles." They were family to us.

Now Joe and Amy Sugar came from New Zealand. They had come to our Mission Station by request. We had the large bungalow and practiced the same Faith. They had no place assigned to them so requested that they be able to serve along with my mother and father in Lakhimpur. They had two sons, David and John, the same age as my sister and I. That was great. We didn't attend the same school in the mountains but our vacations were at the same time.

My dad was happy for Joe Sugar's help in the Work. Dad had been handed the responsibility of chairmanship of the Assembly of God Mission which necessitated considerable paperwork with our headquarters in the United States as well as the Indian Government. It was good to have the Sugar's alternate with us when it came to our usual village evangelism along the border. They could use our tents and camping equipment when Dad had to be in town as we were that particular last week in February.

One afternoon we caught the sound of the old "touring car" coming in the distance. I remember running out to greet David and John thinking, "Oh goody! Now we will have them to play with again!" They drove in the gate slowly and on around to the back of the house. Something unusual was happening. There were no waving arms in greeting, no tooting of the horn, just slow progress until they came to a stop. There was a cot across the back of the car and on it was strapped what appeared to be a bundle of clothes. Only John and David shared the passenger seat next to Uncle Joe who was driving. Where was Auntie Amy?

As we all pressed around, Joe gave us the sad news. Auntie Amy had died of a heart attack two nights before. There was no medical help way out there in the jungle camp. They had made immediate preparations for bringing her body back to Lakhimpur for burial where there was a small plot for a Christian Cemetery.

By sunrise they had reached the big river where they had to await a "ferry." The small boat was scarcely as wide as the car was long and was approached by two six inch wide planks. Uncle Joe had to steer the car slowly up this loosely placed contrivance to keep the wheels from slipping off. There were only four inches of "deck" left behind the rear tires, just enough to jam a brick in front and behind the four wheels. Of course, there were no guardrails and only one man with a twenty-foot bamboo pole to push the craft into the muddy, swirling water.

The abundant winter rains had made the river twice its normal size and the far bank was nowhere to be seen. It was an horrific ride trying to keep everything from sliding off, while the sun beat down mercilessly. By afternoon the "skipper" located a place he thought he could unload, but the road was nowhere in sight.

Getting the car off the ferry was just as precarious as driving it onboard had been. The boys had to be the eyes guiding Daddy Joe down the narrow boards onto the wet sandy bank, then up the steep slopes to level ground. How thankful they were to have made it safely!

They soon came across a tiny thatch tea stall that made them hot "chai" (very sweet, spicy tea and buffalo milk cooked together) and chappatis, an Indian flat bread baked on coals. After pouring the last precious can of petrol into the tank, they climbed aboard and started to go on. Evening was approaching and they were still far from Lakhimpur. In India, in those days, it was the law that you must bury or cremate the dead the same day of their death.

Uncle Joe told us how God had sustained them. As night approached they sat in their seats, quoted Scripture verses, slept if they could, and chased hungry jackals away who had undoubtedly been attracted by the scent of Auntie Amy. They spoke little and cried much as morning dawned and they bore their precious cargo homeward. Not having signposts, they took a wrong turn that cost them three hours of backtracking. By noon Uncle Joe recognized where they were and the weary, heavy-hearted travelers reached the mission compound by afternoon.

We were all shocked and saddened to hear their account. Dad and Uncle Joe lost no time in locating and sawing boards to make a coffin while Mom brought out a white sheet (tacked inside the box) to make it look nice.

While preparations were underway for the funeral, Auntie Amy was laid out in my room, a smallish office room off the main bedroom. The boys and Joe came in and discussed who should remove her wedding ring. Uncle Joe was too overwhelmed with grief to do it and asked if I would do it for them. Neither of the boys wanted the job.

I was ten years old and wanted to be helpful. I had already given up my small treasured bottle of California Poppy perfume to sprinkle all around as the odor was approaching unbearable. It had done little to mask the smell. She had been exposed to two days of hot sun on her un-embalmed body.

"Sure," I said, "I'll be glad to take her ring off for you." I was trying to be brave! No one else offered.

Gradually I loosened the ring. As I leaned over her and tried to pull it off her finger, Aunt Amy suddenly sat straight up, opened her mouth, and disgorged a river of her stomach contents all over me before falling back to her prone position! How do you put into words what I felt at that moment? I was petrified! So were John and David and my sister Hope and younger brother Bob, and we bolted for the door. I did not recover from that fright for years. I was too shaken to attend her funeral an hour later and my mother didn't make me go!

Auntie Amy is in Heaven now. When I get there myself, I am sure we will laugh about the time she scared us kids out of our wits!

— Chapter 4—

The Most Embarrassing Moment of My Entire Life!

It was February on the Atlantic Ocean. We had just left Calcutta, India, in a freighter bound for the USA. With my father recovering from typhus, the low key voyage promised to be a time of rest and rejuvenation for him. Very few people ever survived typhus so we were very thankful to God that we still had him with us. In those days there was no cure. In fact, I have never heard of one. He had visited a remote village in north Kheri District to bring them the Good News of the Gospel. In polite tradition he had been offered a charpai on which to sit. This is a low woven string bed. From this position he spoke to the crowd of villagers that had gathered and were squatting down on their haunches around him, waiting patiently for his words, as was their custom.

The meeting went well. After being offered some hot chai in an earthenware matka, he took his leave. He had left some tracts with the headman who would read them to everyone later. This man was the only one that could read in the whole village. It was then they told him the cot he had been sitting on for the meeting had belonged to an uncle that had died just two days previous, of typhus!

When "Nurse Mom" heard this, she checked up on the rare disease. It was generally transmitted by a bed bug's bite. Dad had plenty of them! When the incubation period had elapsed, he became ill. We took him to the mountains where there were some missionary doctors. We were all put in strict quarantine. Giving him care and comfort medicine along with much prayer was all we could do. He had a high fever and was delirious for days. There was not much hope given for his survival but our God intervened. After a number of weeks he began to revive and slowly gained strength. The local doctors took his blood to use to make serum as antidotes for others. Our own missionary's daughter, Evelyn Snyder, came down with a disease similar to Typhus and Dad's blood was given in transfusion and she too survived.

Now months later we were ready to go on furlough after 7 1/2 years on the field. Dad was still very weak but looking forward to seeing his mother and father and all his family once again. The six of us in our own family were the only passengers on board the freighter and enjoyed the run of the ship. The crew was pleasant and took us kids all over the vessel. We saw the engine room, the bridge, prow and poop decks, the holds for the cargo, the galley, and even the "crow's nest, which was my favorite spot. It was a long climb up the tall ladder to the top of the tall mast. At nine years of age, I decided I wanted to become a sailor!

The chef on board made lovely meals for us in the tiny dining room. The head baker produced delicious pastries we had never imagined existed. He delighted in asking our favorite foods.

We had gone from Calcutta, down the muddy Hoogly River and out into the Indian Ocean. We then went south, down around Ceylon, (now Sri Lanka) across a large expanse of ocean to the Red Sea, through the Suez Canal and the Mediterranean Sea. We docked at many ports along the way to unload and load cargoes of every sort. Sometimes the weather was good but often we hit storms. We kids got very good at remaining upright while the ship listed in every direction.

After passing through the Strait of Gibraltar, weather was fair for some days then abruptly changed. Our small vessel bobbed and dipped and rolled continually and nosed down into the mighty waves.

Mom and Dad had a lovely large cabin. The four of us kids spent hours sprawled on their cabin floor playing Monopoly or Pit. We couldn't walk outside any more for the storms had grown stronger. The next day was going to be Mom's birthday when an idea hit me. It would be so nice to surprise her with a birthday cake!

I angled my way down the narrow passageway to the chef's galley, holding myself up with my hands on opposite walls as the ship did its up and down and sideways dance. The good baker listened to my plea and assured me he would produce a humdinger to remember. No truer words were ever spoken!

The storm grew worse and the Captain advised us through the intercom to stay off the decks and confine our activities to our cabins. Our ship's rudder broke which helped to upset us further. We lay on the floor in the folk's cabin and couldn't even manage Monopoly while our parents kept to their bunks, held in by the raised side panels. It was so rough! That night we dragged our bedding into their room and did our best to sleep but rolled all over. It became quite a game.

Morning finally came and we gave Mom birthday cards we had each contrived on the ship's stationery.

Dad wrote one too. Mom was pleased even though seasick. No one felt like breakfast! The steward brought us coffee and milk which was hard to keep from spilling.

Soon there was a knock on the door. When we yelled, "Come in," it was the baker, with his "humdinger to remember." He had outdone himself and presented me with the promised two layered gorgeous cake tall with cream in swirls and flowers and candy sparkles all over with "HAPPY BIRTHDAY MOM" around the bottom layer. He had thought of everything, even a knife and forks and plates.

I thanked him profusely for it was truly a work of art. We put it on the dresser because it had little raised guardrails around it, presumably for use in storms at sea! We all looked at the beautiful cake. But "look" was all we could manage. We sang "Happy Birthday" to Mom but couldn't persuade her to take a bite. She simply groaned and turned over. We decided to wait in hopes that calmer seas would make us more amenable to indulge in the sweet confection. Even the next day there was no let up in the storm and our little freighter bobbed like a cork in the wild winds and waves. We didn't feel like eating anything, much less, a sweet cake!

What should we do with it? We didn't want to offend the kind baker who had so lovingly made such a beautiful production. But how could we get rid of it to ease our consciences? The room steward would find it if we put it in the wastebasket. We were not allowed on deck to toss it overboard. Ah! The porthole over our sofa would work! No one volunteered to do the terrible deed. Since I had ordered it, it fell to me to toss it. It should go out the porthole over the narrow two foot deck outside and into the ocean for some lucky fish!

So I managed to hold it carefully and balanced myself quite well in front of the porthole. My brother Bob opened the porthole and secured it with the dangling chain and hook. One enormous heave and out it went, straight into the face of a passerby on the narrow deck! My heart sank. In fact I would have welcomed death when we saw who it hit. It was the ship's baker!! What could I say? How could I explain? Where could I hide the rest of the two weeks it took to reach New York?

The pain in my heart is as strong today, 70 years later, as on that awful day. I know God put it into his heart to understand and forgive but my embarrassment was total!

— Chapter 5—

"Hi, You on the Other Elephant"
(How Sam and I met)

Convention was over. "Convention" was always a special occasion on the mission field. It was the once a year time when all the missionaries in our ranks got together at some mission station for Spiritual refreshing, business meetings, fun, and fellowship. We always traveled somewhere by train or car and lived in tents around a building large enough to accommodate sixty or seventy people for eating and meeting. Many children came, too, if the parents could not fine suitable friends with whom to leave them.

In our family there were four kids and that entailed considerable expense for train tickets. More often than not, two of us would accompany our folks and two would stay with friends. The next year the other two would go and the others remain. If the journey was long we went by train (third class). I remember asking my dad why we had to travel third class instead of second or first class. Without a blink he replied, "Because there isn't any fourth!" We understood such reasoning as everything we ever did was governed by expense! Not that we suffered, but we did everything the cheapest possible way.

The year I finished my junior year in High School, my sister Hope had just graduated and so was taken along to Convention since she would soon be leaving for the States. It was her turn anyway! My brother, Bob, and I stayed home with the McKelvies, missionaries from another mission who were staying at our mission station.

The party returned from the convention full of happy details of the wonderful week of activities and meetings and eating, making me envious. One detail I remember best was what my sister told me about a young man who also attended. His name was Sam Beckdahl, the son of Scandinavian missionaries. He was a tall, blond, blue eyed athlete with a bass baritone singing voice that had wowed the whole convention with renditions of "The Old Rugged Cross," and "Amazing Grace." He even sang "Old Man River" like Paul Robson used to sing. She talked so much about him, I grumbled, "Why do I always have to miss the good stuff?"

It was nearly time for our vacation to end. School would be starting in the Himalayan Mountains on March 1st. You see, school started in March and ended in November when all the children would go down to the plains to be with their parents during the cool months of the year.

One of our lady missionaries (Mrs. Ruby Nicodem) was having a birthday that last week. The Nicodems also lived on the border of Nepal as we did, but it took two days by train between our mission stations. There were six Nicodem children and they were our friends. Since Bob and I did not get to go to Convention, we were invited to Rupaidhia to help celebrate Aunt Ruby's birthday.

On arrival the Nicodem boys came to the station to take us to their house. There we were informed that the "D.C." (District Commissioner) had arranged for an elephant to pick us up the next morning to go into the jungle to hunt down a marauding tiger that was decimating the villagers' buffaloes and goats. Since I could handle a gun, I was welcomed. There would also be another elephant with hunters and guns.

Bright and early found us scrambling up the tail of the elephant and perching atop our pachyderm conveyance, padding swiftly into the jungle. It was exhilarating to breathe in the morning smells of the damp jungle and listen to the choirs of morning birds singing their praises to the Almighty. My own heart fairly burst with joy in this green cathedral. We must have rhythmically and silently traveled an hour when we arrived at a small clearing where the other elephant was awaiting our arrival. The "D. C." alighted from his beautiful beast to come over and welcome us and tell us that he had the good fortune to get a very good hunter, Samuel Beckdahl, from Nanpara, thirty miles away, to join the hunt as well.

My heart did a flip. Our elephants approached each other. I couldn't believe it! Here was that gorgeous hunk I would never get to see, and all my tongue could utter was, "Hi!"

The hunt got under way. Plans were made about tracking and beating the jungle and hopefully pushing the tiger where he was somewhat confined and could be shot. The "Shikari," an Indian hunting guide, on my elephant readied his rifle, as did I and Frank Nicodem, while Sam and the "D.C." did likewise. We were off.

It is an absolute joy to ride a well trained hunting elephant that knows when to make a noise with his feet and when to approach silently. A good elephant will stand absolutely like a statue when facing an angry tiger so the hunter on top of his back can get a true shot! This is especially remarkable in that tigers often make frontal attacks.

We saw fleeting deer and sambar, nilguy, and a few black buck but the hunt was anticlimactic. The elusive cat didn't show. But I didn't care. I "got" my tiger, and he "got" me. We became friends even though we had to return to our own mission stations after celebrating Aunt Ruby's birthday, and then return to our separate boarding schools the following week. Nicodems and Merians went back to Woodstock School in Landour, Mussoorie and Sam went to his British Military School in Darjeeling.

We corresponded. I finished my senior year at Woodstock and graduated two months after my sixteenth birthday. Then I headed for the States and college as most American missionary kids did.

Although Sam had been accepted in Central Bible College in Springfield, Missouri, the British government had other plans for him. Because his parents had failed to register him with the Norwegian or Danish Embassies at his birth, he was immediately inducted into the British Indian Army as the war was on. He already had military training so was soon assigned a command of Nepali Gurka Troops. Thus began his great love of Nepali people and six years of active duty, at the front lines in Burma, then Iran, Iraq, and elsewhere. God miraculously spared his life many times.

I went on to college in the States. We "courted" by mail for five years. I also worked in a defense plant and saved money for my return to India because Sam had asked me to be his wife!

— Chapter 6—

Beginnings

I had received a visa for reentry to India on "Compassionate Grounds," to marry Sam. But the journey during war time had taken so long, (four months) that my visa had expired right after I got there and Sam had been shipped to PAIFORCE, (Persia and Iraq Force,) and we could not get married. I was told that I would have to go back to America. That was easier said than done! All my money was gone. Prayer was my only recourse. I have found that God never fails to make a way when His children ask.

I wrote to the top general of the British Army and lay my dilemma before him. I asserted that after all the British had issued my visa and now I couldn't use it as they had shipped Sam out of the country. I had no finances for a return to the USA. Thankfully, the general cabled Sam's Commanding Officer in Persia with this message,"This Officer will proceed on leave, forthwith!—General Aukenleck."

Sam's C.O. was outraged that someone had gone over his head sending one of his officers on leave. Comply, he did, however. He didn't dare do otherwise!

We were married in Kellogg Memorial Church at the top of Landour, Mussoorie, where the eternal snows witnessed our vows. It was July and the middle of the monsoons. But July 24th saw the sun come out to the amazement of everybody. How good of God to give us sunshine for our special day. I carried a beautiful bouquet of white gladiolas. Missionary, Verena Rich was my Maid of Honor and Sam's friend, Paul Schoonmaker stood with him as Best Man.

Missionaries came to our wedding from many distant stations, about one hundred of them. We saw many of our Indian friends. My Mom and Dad and brother Walter were there. There was one off note that was difficult to understand. Sam's parents did not attend. His mother had tried to make him promise he would not marry until he was twenty-five years old. It upset her that he was still twenty-four at the time of our nuptials. Years later I came to see that her determination on issues that mattered to her helped give fire to her drive in good things as well, but that hurt us at the time.

It was a beautiful wedding. I had brought my wedding gown from America and carried it everywhere for months. That hatbox had seen rough treatment when it fell to the bottom of one ship's hold when the cargo net of the boom broke and sent all the luggage it held to the bottom with a crash. I was watching from the deck and saw my precious hatbox lifted high then dropped and spilled all over the floor of the ship. I can still recall the sick feeling that came over me. I ran down and pleaded with the stevedores to let me go down to locate my belongings. It took tenacity to persuade them. I promised I'd pray for them if they would grant me permission. Strangely enough, that did it and I did pray, audibly, as they stood around stunned!

I located everything! One small disaster: I had a little bottle of liquid shoe polish for my sandals. It broke! I had a Herculean task getting that white stuff out of all the garments. If only I had thought to wrap it in plastic! Hindsight is always best!

To my eyes, the reception was fabulous! Our missionary ladies had decorated the Community Center with ferns and flowers of the monsoon varieties. Our Muslim friends who were Persian Carpet dealers had brought their choicest carpets and covered the entire hall floor with exquisite rugs of gorgeous wool and silk. It was an act of pure love. Some of the Hindu venders of baked goodies brought sandwiches and sweets. I had made a three-tiered fruit cake made with all kinds of fruit I had collected on my long journey and decorated it lovingly before learning that Sam had been sent out of the country. I had to think how best to keep it fresh. So I "shot" it with brandy to preserve it until Sam could come back to India. It kept beautifully and many of our missionaries asked for the recipe, not knowing the secret of its flavor. As far as I know, America is the only place where brides have white cakes for their weddings.

Sam performed his first husbandly act when I leaned over to slice the wedding cake, the top tiny button at the back of my gown popped open followed by the dozens of tiny buttons down to my waist. He successfully put me together again much to the amusement of all our guests.

Oh, the speeches! How I wish we had the capability to record them! This dear family of mission friends had watched us grow from infancy. Several made mention that they had prayed for Sam when his mother had sent word she had a tumor. That tumor eventually turned out to be a twelve-pound baby boy! Until she was taken to a local "hospital" by the Nicodems, their closest neighbors, when Mom Beckdahl was having severe stomach cramps, and got there just in time to have the baby, would she believe she was pregnant. Fortunately, Aunt Ruby had guessed her "problem" and came armed with a few baby clothes and blankest from her own two month old son, Jack. To the day Sam died, the missionaries we knew back then kidded him about praying for him when he was a tumor! God bless them!

After the reception, a "dandi" (palanquin carried on the shoulders of four coolies) carried me through Landour Bazaar. From there a rickshaw sped us five miles to where we spent our one week honeymoon at a boarding house in Happy Valley, Mussoorie. It was wonderful. We spent days hiking around the chakars (mountain roads) and hiked to Kempty Falls down in the valley, three times. No cars plied the roads in those years. We frequently stopped to buy mangos which we took back to the hotel. There we sat on opposite sides of a big tin tub eating the delicious fruit with the juice all over our faces and running down our arms and off our elbows.

We strolled through the bazaar talking to Nepalese, Tibetans, and Gharwalis and renewed acquaintances with many people and shopkeepers we had known in earlier years. That happy week went so quickly and brought our short but fantastic time together to a close.

Sam had to go back to Persia and the war, but now I didn't have to leave India. Woodstock School needed an Art and Home Economics teacher and I was asked to fill in. Here in my old school where I had attended from Kindergarten through High School it was my joy to teach!

In eight months when Sam finally came back to India we were stationed in Allahabad and Benaris. I enjoyed being an army wife and was very proud of Sam.

He always looked great. He was a superb athlete and looked wonderful with his men on parade! He loved those men. They would often bring food from the Indian kitchen because they knew how we both loved it. Most of all he enjoyed the special camaraderie he shared with the nationals.

Sam had now served in the British Indian Army for six years. I was with him the last two. He received his notification of demobilization. At last, Central Bible College was in his sights again.

A train took us to Calcutta where we embarked on the freighter, "SS President Grant." The trip took us six weeks to reach Boston Harbor. It was Christmas Eve and snowing hard. We took the night train to new York. Oh! Such luxury! We now had blankets but our ears were cold. At Macys we went in and Sam asked a salesperson to direct us to where we might purchase "she" caps. The kind gentleman immediately sent us to the lady's department on the next floor. I took over translating Sam's good "English" to "American" from then on. ("She" is the way the Europeans and British pronounce the word "ski.")

A week later found us in Springfield, Missouri where God had originally prompted Sam to attend Bible College. Our first child was due in a couple of months. Not knowing whether we would be welcoming a girl or a boy, we usually prayed for "Daniel Esther."

On May 31st, 1947, our ten-pound bouncing baby boy arrived bringing great joy into our lives. Although we had dedicated this baby to God much earlier, he was presented to the Lord in dedication by Uncle Ralph Riggs, in Central Assembly in Springfield, Missouri.

Daniel Frederick was 17 months old when Esther

Elise was born in September 1948 while we were still in Springfield. Soon after that we left for India. Elizabeth Anne joined the family in May of 1953. She was born in Landour Community Hospital in Mussoorie. Our youngest, Joseph Christian, was born during our first furlough back in Springfield in March of 1955.

These were the children God gave to us. Though they are only just mentioned here, their lives were of utmost importance to us. There is a chapter on each one of them later in this book. Our lives as missionaries affected each one differently. We are all complex individuals and come with different gifts, talents, and personalities. But that is what makes a family mosaic so interesting. Our family is no exception.

— Chapter 7—
Ali Baba and the Forty Thieves

During the second world war I was separated from my fiancé by the Atlantic Ocean, the Mediterranean and Red Seas and the Indian Ocean. Sam had been inducted into the British Indian Army after graduating from High School in Darjeeling. He had been about to leave India for Bible Collage in the United States when war broke out, canceling his plans. His Scandinavian parents had failed to claim Norwegian or Danish citizenship for him at birth so he had no birthright papers exempting him from army induction. Fortunately for me, my parents had registered my birth at the American Consulate so I had dual citizenship, and I left India to pursue further education outside of India.

The war was pressing and the Japanese had invaded Burma with the intentions of taking over India, a favorite British possession. Sam saw grueling action-packed years of combat leading Nepali troops in Burma before the tide finally turned and he had only handfuls of brave, stalwart Gurkas left in his regiment. They were repatriated to India.

During these four years our courtship was entirely by mail. There were times when no mail got through to the front lines or out of the chaos to the outside world. For six months when I was in Taylor University, Upland, Indiana, I heard nothing. It was rumored to his parents in India, he had been captured or killed. I kept writing, in hope, until one happy day I received word that he had received a whole pouch of my letters. Neither he or his men were permitted to communicate where they were located.

That is not the point of this tale! Now that he was back in India we started making our plans for marriage. Wasn't it Scottish poet Bobby Burns who said, "The best laid plans of mice and men oft go astray."? Stray they did! But hopes of soon being together kept us probing every possibility. Wartime was not conducive to giving favors to civilians. My pleas for a visa to go back to India finally paid off. Some kind high placed Army officer issued me a six-month visa on "compassionate grounds." That was all I needed!

No time was wasted in getting my savings together to buy the ticket. But no travel agency would sell me one! "Didn't I know that there was a war going on?" Finally a Portuguese shipping firm agreed to take me on board their freighter as far as Lisbon, Portugal. They were also taking a bunch of missionaries, including my parents and younger brother, Walter, who couldn't get tickets elsewhere.

I knew exactly what I wanted to take Sam for a wedding present. Four years on the front lines and nothing at his parent's very rural dwelling meant that he would have very little decent civilian attire. So I bought him some real American clothes. This would be a sure hit as everyone outside the USA yearned for the smartness of real American clothing. I bought a nice jacket, slacks, shirts, ties and even underwear. I had him trace his foot on paper so I knew his shoe and sock size. My excitement grew and I even bought a suitcase to hold it all. Now I had my suitcase, his suitcase, and a hat box which held my wedding dress, my sister's veil, some underwear, white sandals and a long slip. The dress had cost me twenty-six dollars! It would have been a bargain at any price because one could scarcely find one for sale at all in New York during the war.

 I sent off for my passport. It didn't come and didn't come. I didn't know what the hold up could possibly be. While awaiting passage, I stayed with my parents, brother, and other missionaries and prayed with them. The Lord whispered a word in my heart, "Behold I have set before thee an open door and no man shall shut it." It was a rock under my feet and I held on tight. The day came when we were told to go to Philadelphia from where the ship would sail. But where was my passport?

 The pier was crowded. My heart was heavy as everyone went up the gangplank. I sent my three precious pieces of luggage up the gangplank with everyone else. Soon the pier was almost empty and I was standing alone. "But You promised me, Lord, that no one would shut the door," I reminded Him in near despair.

 They were pulling up the gang plank when a uniformed runner came up and asked if I was Ruth Merian. When assured that I was he handed me the package from Washington. He hadn't let me down!! From the railing on the deck above came clapping and shouts to let the gang plank back down. I literally ran up it, thanking the Lord at each gallop!

 Lisbon was interesting, We lived in a "pension" on the 5th floor. We discovered "with running water" meant you had to run to the end of the hall to retrieve some from a tap. "With breakfast" meant a plate of hard rolls and coffee for all of us to share. Our maid spoke

English. It was too bad that all she could say was "Shleep well." This was her greeting early morning, at night or if we met her in the hall anytime! We spent the time the best we could and walked daily to the office to learn if another ship had come in to take us on the next lap of our journey. We watched marble sculptors making statues. We looked in shops endlessly.

Mr. Pennington, one of the missionaries bound for Africa, needed some saddle soap to waterproof his boots. We all went into the shop and he tried to explain to the salesman in his limited Portuguese vocabulary, by miming and vigorously "washing" his hands; by rubbing his shoes. and acting as if he was galloping on a horse, with no success. In desperation he turned to us and said, "Maybe they don't know what saddle soap is!" With that the salesman said in perfect English, "Why didn't you tell me you wanted Saddle Soap?" We had a good laugh then and many times since!

A month passed in Lisbon and finally we were on our way to a very southern port in Portugal where a British coastal cutter picked us up and crowded us all into the lounge of the tiny vessel. But we were ecstatic. We were given huge slices of white bread with strawberry jam, not the hard rolls we had eaten for five weeks in Lisbon. Instead of fish, which had come whole on the plate, with open eyes and the tail tucked into its mouth, we had meat and potatoes! No longer was everything cooked in olive oil. Indeed, every music box or band seemed to play the same tunes and we jokingly dubbed them the "olive oil tunes." Familiar is something very comforting at times!

In this wee lounge some of us slept on tables, some in hammocks hung above the tables and some of the elderly among us, under the tables. There were twenty of us in our group and we gratefully accepted the kind hospitality of this British Cutter. They took us to Gibraltar under complete blackout.

On Gibraltar my brother Walter and I roamed all over "The Rock." Small cars drove everywhere. "The Rock" was a genius of fortification, completely tunneled with hidden openings for gun emplacements. There were well equipped shops and an amazing hospital. Walt and I were taken down and through some of the docked submarines by two of the "Limey" sailors with whom we had become friends. What an adventure! The tiny living quarters make my present motor home look like a spacious mansion.

A French vessel, the "Marseilles" picked us up and under strict blackout, took us through the Mediterranean Sea to Aden. This ship was the scariest I had ever encountered. It rolled from side to side so violently that the doors were locked to the lounge unbeknown to me while I was out on deck. The ship went over so far that my feet got wet while I held on to the railings for dear life! I almost despaired of its righting itself and I remember preparing myself to meet Jesus! The storm finally abated and I was able to attract the attention of a crewmember that got the door opened for me. Inside the scene was chaotic. Our missionaries had been tossed and rolled from side to side. I remember seeing sedate Miss King tangled in chair legs and much bruised.

We were so glad to reach Aden and board the huge British troop ship, P&O Line, the "Otronto." There were thousands of soldiers on board. We were billeted in cabins wherever there was a place to squeeze us in. We were all split up . Some were in 1st, 2nd, and 3rd class accommodations. We couldn't mingle. It was Christmas Eve. One of our group, Harriet Williams, and I decided we would like to do something for the troops on board. We requested permission to sing, from the bridge, to all the men milling on the open decks below. To this day my heart skips a beat when I recall the thrill we had as the voice over the loudspeaker told the troops to be quiet and listen. God surely enlarged our lungs and singing capacity as, in the semi-darkness, we began singing "Oh Holy Night." We sang all the verses and when it was over there was silence, then thunderous applause from below. No super star could have ever received a greater ovation and thrill than we did that night on the bridge of the "Otronto." In fact it is the only applause I ever got for singing but it reverberates in my heart these sixty years later!

Oh yes, what about "Ali Baba?" Zigzagging through the Suez Canal and the Red Sea and out into the Indian Ocean under complete darkness, we arrived in Bombay five days later without German or Japanese interference. Going up country by train for two days and nights we arrived safely at our mission station in Lakhimpur. The journey had taken so long that my visa soon expired and Sam had been sent overseas to Persia where he and his men were detailed to guard the communication wires into Russia, a US and British ally. These wires were copper and were constantly being stolen by thieves who were difficult to apprehend. This was "Ali Baba's Territory."

Not finding Sam in India I wrote to the top general of the British army for help. I was going to be sent back to the United States if I did not get married. I could not leave because I had no money! General Aukenleck came through with a cable to Sam's commanding officer and even though it angered his CO to be over-stepped, Sam was sent back to India immediately.

We were married in the Kellogg Memorial Church on top of Mussoorie. It was a beautiful day. On our honeymoon I gave him the suitcase of American clothes. He was struck dumb with pleasure and appreciation. After our short honeymoon, he had to leave to go back to PAIFORCE (Persia and Iraq Force) clutching his new suitcase.

Now, living in a tent in the desert was no place to hide cherished possessions. Ali Baba's thieves were notorious in their methods. It was not unusual to awaken to find all your belongings gone. Men were ordered to dig a trench and sleep on their rifles. Clever thieves would then tickle them enough to change their positions and silently slide out their guns! Next they were ordered to chain their guns to themselves! That proved to be a deterrent because they couldn't go off with gun and man! Sam took every precaution with his belongings. His gun and now his suitcase were chained to him. One morning he awoke with the sun shining in his eyes. The whole tent was gone. His gun and EMPTY suitcase were still chained to his wrist!

Sam told me later how his CO had lost his jeep from right outside his tent. They followed the jeep by its tracks being pushed away from camp. Suddenly there were no more tracks in the sand. The jeep had been completely cannibalized, taken apart piece by piece, and carted away on the backs of donkeys!

SO, ALI BABA AND HIS BAND OF FORTY

THIEVES WERE STILL VERY MUCH ALIVE AND WELL, AND, MIGHT I ADD, SUCCESSFUL!

Sam as a baby.

Sam in Nepali outfit with
mom and dad

Sam & his mother and dad on furlough during World War II.

Sam as he was inducted into the British Indian Army in April 1941.

Grandma Elise Merian

از الیاس ناظم علی ناظم لکھیم پوری، تحصیل بھیم پور کھیڑی

تاریخ ۱۷ ستمبر سنہ ۱۹۵۸ء

مسٹر میریں کی اعلیٰ شخصیت

دنیا کی بعض سب لوگ ہستیاں ایسی ہوتی ہیں جو اپنے صداقت پردازانہ اور برد بار طرز عمل کا خود بخود اعتراف کرا لیتی ہیں۔ دنیا ایک آزمائش اور امتحان کی جگہ ہے۔ یہاں کسی کی ذاتی شہرت و اقتدار انسان کے دلوں میں اپنا گھر نہیں بنا سکتا۔ بلکہ رحم دلی، مساوات، انسانی ہمدردی وہ اوصاف انسانی جوہر ہیں جو اس کو ارتقا کی انتہائی بلندیوں پر پہنچا دیتے ہیں۔

مسٹر ایف۔ اے۔ میریں (Mr. F. A. Merian) ان دل والی ہستیوں میں سے ہیں جنہوں نے نفسیات انسانی کا بنظر غائر مطالعہ کیا ہو۔ وہ سمجھتے ہیں کہ سب انسان آپس میں برابر ہیں۔ آپ کا شیوہ ہے ہر غریب و امیر سے یکساں برتاؤ کرنا۔ غریبوں کے دکھے ہوئے دلوں کی تسکین کے لئے ایسی ہرگز بزیدہ ہستیوں کی زبان سے نکلے ہوئے الفاظ مرہم کا کام کرتے ہیں۔ ان کے ہر فعل اور قول میں شرافت نفس جھلکتی رہتی ہے۔

مجھے بذات خود دو قتاً فوقتاً جناب موصوف سے ملاقات کا شرف حاصل ہوتا رہتا ہے اور میں اپنی ان ملاقاتوں کے دوران میں جن نتائج پر پہنچ سکا ہوں۔ ان کے پیش نظر و شوق کے ساتھ یہ کہا جاسکتا ہے۔ کہ مسٹر ممدوح نہایت شریف النفس۔ رحم دل۔ اور ہمدرد انسان ہیں اور غریب سے غریب اشخاص بھی آپ کی ہرگز بزیدہ شخصیت سے بلا جھجک نیفیاب ہوتے ہیں۔ آپ ان تمام انسانی صفات کے حامل ہیں جو امتیازی شخصیتوں کے لئے از بس ضروری ہیں۔

آج کی ضرورت ہے جنرل حکمت نے ما ہے۔

صاحب ممدوح کا عقیدت مند
ناظم علی

Missionary, Mr. Merian
A Man of God

There are very few selfless personalities in this world whose truthfulness and sincerity is acknowledged by everyone. This world is an Examination Hall and everyone has to pass their tests here. It is is not personal distinction or the wealth of a man that enchants people's hearts, but hearts are only won by sympathy, benevolence and equality, which are the greatest achievements of human character.

Mr. F. A. Merian is one of those sympathetic persons who loves his fellowman — not acknowledging the superiority of the rich over the poor. His gentle and encouraging words to the poorest of us, has been the greatest solace to us. The nobility of his words and action have shown us God.

TRANSLATION OF NEWSPAPER ARTICLE FROM LAKHIMPUR, KHERI, U.P. INDIA

Written by Mr. Nazim Ali
(A prominent Muslim in Lakhimpur)

Our early pets were pups, goats and an orphaned deer "Bitsy." She became so tame and learned many tricks. For instance, she would go around the table begging a morsel from each of us until my dad would give a whistle and she would spring high over us and the table, landing squarely by the door to the shrieks of unsuspecting guests.

Hope and Ruth with pets

Mom dispensing ointment and love in the villages and praying with each patient.

Woodstock School in the Himalayan Mountains where we were sent to boarding school and attended from kindergarten through high school.

This is the village where Dad contracted typhus.

A ferry like this carried the Sugar's body
across the wide river.

FAREWELL ADRESS

TO

Miss Ruth Elise Merian

A. G. Mission
LAKHIMPUR
Distt *KHERI.*
U. P. India

Dear Miss Merian,

We your Lakhimpur friends and fellow Christians have gathered here this afternoon to say good bye to you. Though we are glad to know that you are going to your mother land, but still our hearts are made heavy at the thought of this separation from us, because after all Lakhimpur is your birth place.

Your parent came to this Town, before your birth and so we have watched you grow from infancy. Your smiling face has endeared you to us all you have been a great help in our sorrows and in our joys. We will miss you so much for Badminton and many other activities. Partings are always sad. but every cloud has its silver lining and so we are not saying goodbye to you but "au revoir" as the sentiments of philippine bid to St. Paul "Come back to philippie" and so we shall always hope that you will return to us.

We not only believe but know that you loved us, you were born in India and you know us well that we are knit together in the bonds of calvary.

We pray god bless you and give you a safe and happy Voyage and bring you back to us again

We are
your friends & welwishers
of this District.

Ruth as Sam's bride on July 24, 1945.

The knot is tied.

Sam and Ruth with Dad and Mom Merian and brother Walter.

Our wedding day. We were married in Kellogg Memorial Church in Landeur Mussoorie in the Himalayan Mountains. Paul Schoonmaker was Best Man. Verena Rich was Maid of Honor.

After the wedding Ruth was carried in a "dandi" through town.

Duchess caring for Beth.

Dan and his 3 "loves," Duchess, his sling shot and sister Esther —in that order.

Dan and his beloved dog Duchess

Duchess at ten months old — ever watchful

Our family heading out for camp along the border of Nepal.

Starting the day with worship is a priority before the daily activities.

Tharu women listened to the radio and wanted to know how the people got inside to speak to us.

The Tharu tribe is matriarchal and actually listened to Ruth speak, but got up and walked away when Sam spoke. I enjoyed the change!

Sam sat and watched when the children had their baths in the river.

Friends carrying a sick member for us to pray for.

Breakfast in camp was often a public affair as Tharus were curious to see how and what we ate.

Tharus Bride and Groom.

Dan and Joe with some of their Tharus pals.

Our children enjoying a "Machan" used by farmers to call out at night to protect their fields from deer eating their crops.

Beth and Joe enjoyed petting the big cat now.

Looks tame now, but it was a maneater and marauded the villager's cattle and children.

"Mela" Days. Religious gatherings.

More "Mela" Days in Kheri District.

The snake charmer came to call out the snakes in our house.

The well on the compound where the big snake appeared and scared Beth & Joe away from playing there.

— Chapter 8—

"And Balaam's Donkey Spoke"

God opened that donkey's mouth and he spoke! Whoever heard of a donkey speaking? God can use even dumb animals to show His power and do the miraculous.

As it was a Mission' requirement, Sam and I had to attend Language School before being permitted full missionary endeavor. We both knew the spoken language from infancy but we had to know how to read and write as well. But this story isn't about language learning.

Since we had to attend classes in the mountains we left our two precious children in the capable hands of an ayah, a native nanny. We left every morning and returned at mid-day. Every noon our white German Shepherd puppy (now six months), bounded up the hill to greet us with lots of licking and tail wagging, followed by Dan and Esther.

This particular noon, no Duchess appeared. We called and called. Where was she and where were the children? Reaching the house, the dudh-walla (the man that brought us milk from his buffaloes down in the valley) informed us that he had seen Danny sitting on a ledge down the mountain with his feet dangling over a steep precipice of maybe 500 feet. "The white dog had its front paws over Budhababa's lap," he said. (Old man little boy, a descriptive name given to Dan because of his white blond hair) "When I tried to get close enough to grab him to safety, the dog would not let me come near," he added.

Our Ayah, with Esther, was high above Dan's perch wringing her hands. "Sahib, he wanted to look down and ran from me too quickly. I couldn't stop him," she wailed.

Dropping our books we rushed to the scene. There was Duchess with her front paws pinning Dan to the narrow ledge. Taking in the situation we stopped calling her. Sam quickly scrambled down the mountainside and reached to grab Dan's shirt and sweater collar. Only then did that noble dog leave her self-appointed perch and Sam was able to slowly pull Dan up and into his arms. If Dan had moved at all, he would have plunged over the edge and been dashed to pieces on the rocks way below.

There was no doubt in our minds at all! The same God who made the mouth of Balaam's donkey speak, is the same God Who gave a six-month-old dog the sense to lie across Dan's lap on that mountainside, and to deafen her ears to our repeated calling.

Duchess was an amazing creature. She was definitely Dan's dog. She displayed unusual attributes. Her protective nature was one of constant wonderment to us. Although fierce in bark and stance, she had a "mother's heart." She adopted many small animals. I remember when a stray baby rabbit hopped over where she lay. I watched her in curiosity as her head quizzically tilted from side to side watching the rabbit. When the little bunny decided to hop away, she got up and actually "corralled" it and lay down with it close to her bosom.

When Duchess had pups, we could put kittens with the litter to share her bounty. She actually adopted baby chicks and a gosling. Even a peacock stayed with her for several months. She was always distressed and sad when any of her "children" would stray and not come back.

She grew old gracefully and was a beloved member of our family. She remained obedient and affectionate. It was furlough time and we hated to leave her. We were in the mountains and some missionary friends came to visit. We were standing in a circle discussing our dilemma about what to do with Duchess. She came and joined us, walked twice around the circle, lay down and died.

Surely God directed even that!

— *Chapter 9* —

Accident on Monkey Boulevard

I had the precious permit hidden in my shoe! The old jeep did a superb creeping tactic as we forged slowly through the heart of Ajhodia towards the grain market.

The day was beastly hot. But our business was very pressing. Verena Rich and I had traveled by jeep 14 miles from Nawabganj and crossed the wide expanse of river on a long bobbing boat bridge. Precariously we climbed the steep sand banks leading to Ajhodia to buy our gunny sack of wheat. A conference convening at our mission had given me the disturbing honor of being the catering committee!

What is hard about bringing home a bag of wheat? That, my friend, is no problem, provided there IS a bag of wheat to get after months of trips to government offices; requisitioning; persuading officials that such wheat was really needed; and filling out forms in quadruplicate. (no copy machines available back then!) The big question had been, would the permit arrive before its expiration date? IT HAD! And tomorrow it was needed!

Now Ajhodia is no ordinary town by anybody's standards. If there is a town in all of India to be considered holy, surely Adhodia's claim topped them all. Here was the sangam (joining) of three sacred rivers. Where else were there thousands of temples and literally thousands of holy men in two square miles? Oxcarts, horse carts, people carts, and bicycles vied with countless pedestrians and cows, chickens and goats for the right of way. And monkeys, thousands of monkeys, swooped down from shop roofs and balconies to grab what they could from passersby or each other. Such din! Unhindered, the sauntering cows and agile monkeys snatched what they wanted from vendors and shops....for wasn't this their holy right?

It happened, like most accidents do, with no warning. The horse that was pulling an ekka (small passenger wagon), directly ahead of us, slipped and sat down. To avoid collision, I swerved to the right and barely connected with the tail end of a long man-pulled cart inching down the wrong side of the road. The jolt did not injure or even scare the man pulling the cart. He couldn't avoid being bumped and pushed constantly on such roads with tangled masses of people, animals and vehicles.

But the bump was a match to the political tinder. Instantly, the jostling crowd turned into a threatening mob. They yelled at us two foreign women devils. They shook their fists and tried to overturn our jeep. I remember humorously, now, that it didn't turn over because people on both sides were lifting their sides simultaneously. We just went up and down and were bounced around. Crazy things happen when people act in frenzy!

In a flash a man dressed in white Ghandi cap and clothes, scrambled onto the jeep hood. He waved his arms and spoke forcefully from his vantage point. His high caste attire and commanding manner quieted the mob.

"Where is the man that was hit?" he demanded.

"Over there, over there!" screamed the angries,

thinking they had found a spokesman for their cause.

"Let him come here," signaled the man. The crowd parted to push the "injured" man to the jeep.

"Now, where are you hurt, my friend?" queried the spokesman. The "thela-wala," obviously enjoying the publicity, couldn't decide where he was hurt. Someone cried, "His head was injured," while another told him his legs were hit. Personally, I felt numb. One look at Verena showed she was frightened, too. Both of us prayed hard.

Without further questions, the white-clad man jumped down, parted the crowd and pulled the fallen horse to its feet. He adjusted the harness straps and pushed the injured man up to the small platform on the conveyance. He then pulled some money from the string pouch at his waist and commanded the driver to take the man to the government hospital nearby. Evidently the amount of money was generous for the driver whipped the horse to a run immediately calling a cheerful equivalent of "Yes, Sir!" before the giver could change his mind.

With that, he announced to the crowd that they should scatter or he would take them all to the police station. He reminded them that he had witnessed the accident, too! The stunned onlookers cooperated immediately. We started to thank our benefactor, but where was he? He was not there! Only an empty spot of ground remained where he had stood two seconds before! Verena and I blinked and looked at each other. Instinctively we bowed our heads, mine over the steering wheel, "Thank you, Lord! We know Your Angel helped us this hour!"

Our spirits soared. We laughed and cried and

praised God audibly! We must have bought the grain and got home safely. I merely recall having a successful conference. But to this day, Verena and I remember and relive the exhilarating details of that "accident on Monkey Boulevard."

— *Chapter 10* —

Bath Time with the Crocks

Bath time is a happy time whether sitting in a lovely porcelain tub with hot and cold water coming out of the spout, or as we often did in a round tin tub in the back part of a tent out in the jungle camp. Or even in a river dividing Nepal and India, where, of course, one must be aware of big hungry crocodiles looking for a juicy morsel of boy or girl!

Much of our work as missionaries took us to these remote areas where river bathing was a necessity. The Biblical admonition to "watch and pray" could easily be advocated as "watch and bathe." We found it absolutely necessary to allow our children into the river with me scrubbing them and Sam sitting on a high spot of the river bank with his rifle cocked and ready.

On several occasions Sam had to fire to protect our little bathers. It was always a game to pull one of these aggressive beasts out onto the bank after they had threatened one of the children but shot in time to rescue them from the fate of many of the village women coming to the edge of the river to fill their water jars or wash their clothes.

After turning the crock over on its back, we would have the job of getting it on the jeep and taking it into camp and then the task of skinning it. That was a difficult job. Crocodile hide is only good on it's underside. The top is impossible to cut. One such beast that Sam dispatched, we cut open the stomach and found women's jewelry. Some was still intact but some partly eaten away by the stomach acid. We found money and earrings! One of them had many tennis ball size eggs inside. They were round and had soft rubber-like shells. The children had fun throwing them at each other! The villagers were always grateful to have the crocodiles nearest their villages taken care of this way because it bought them a measure of safety for a while. They depended on the river for their water, for bathing, washing their clothes, cooking, and drinking. Someone's wife or child getting snatched and pulled under, never to be seen again, happened all too often.

    One such day when I had called for the children to get out of the river to dry off and put on their clean clothes, a man came up to us with a front cycle basket full of tiny tiger cubs! They had been on the jungle path as he had pedaled through. He stopped and picked them up, a very dangerous thing to do if the mother was anywhere near! Obviously, she had gone hunting and these four babies with eyes still closed, had wandered away from where she had left them. He begged me to take the cubs, as he couldn't keep them. So we let each of the kids carry one into camp. There I located a pair of rubber gloves which we used for nipples, mixed up some powdered milk and fed them. They devoured the milk noisily and wanted lots more. I felt so sorry for the mother tiger who must have gone insane losing her babies. The next day we took them to the forest department near the edge of the forest and turned them over to take to some zoo. We heard later that they were sent to Cairo, Egypt, for their zoological gardens.

— *Chapter 11*—

Tiger Tracks

Have you ever traced the tracks of animals in the wild? It is fun. These tracks are called pug marks. If you grow up in India or Africa or any other place where hunting is necessary, or like Daniel Boone, you quickly learn to recognize the differences between animal pugs. It can be important to know whether they are fresh or old marks. You are able to judge the size of an animal by the size of the pugs. For example: You see a pug mark of a wild elephant. If you measure the circumference of its foot print and multiply by 3.5, you can quite accurately predict the height of that elephant!

In our rural evangelistic endeavors on the northern border of India, we generally camped in forest areas near the villages. Often we were begged by the villagers to help them get rid of some big cat that was causing havoc in their region. Their cattle, chickens, or goats were often taken as easy prey by the beasts and thus their livelihood jeopardized. Occasionally, tigers or leopards turned to taking human victims for their food and you can imagine the terror the people lived with when this began in their area! Naturally, as a service of love we tried to help whenever we could. This proved to be a real challenge several times.

One particular time, five village men came near our tent one evening with hands clasped as if in prayer and pleaded for Sam to come to their aid. A tiger had been raiding their village and carting off their paddas (young water buffaloes). No amount of "scaring off" tactics had kept the big cat away. They were desperate.

A plan of action was considered. We knew that most tigers have their own territories they have marked off for themselves by scenting bushes or trees and that they regularly patrol the rounds of their domain. We needed to find out about this tiger's habits.

"Oh, we know where he makes his rounds," one man remarked, " and we can show you, Sahib."

All was arranged for the next evening because it had been four nights since his last kill, and he was due to strike again. Sam and I got ready. He carried the gun. We were taken to the place where there were fresh pug marks in the soft path. It was easy to follow the trail he had just taken. By the size of its tracks it was a large male. I carried pebbles in my hand which I would throw ahead if we weren't certain of his whereabouts. The noise of a thrown pebble might make him show himself before we would get too close for safety.

For about an hour and a half we moved silently and followed his footsteps. Eventually we came back to where we had started. To our surprise, now his tracks were *over* ours! He was tracking *us*! Tigers can be very clever indeed. It was late in the evening and the shadows obscured our vision but we knew his eyes could pierce any darkness. We called off the chase! The hunters were now the hunted! It was time for new tactics.

— *Chapter 12* —

Angels Ride Shotgun

"Madam, you know as well as I do, as soon as that railway carriage is shunted over here and attached to the train, it will be just as bulging as the rest of the compartments. They will sit on you, Madam. Are you prepared to face this?"

"Sir, I am prepared for ANYTHING! I must go to Delhi—-today," I said, but inside myself I was chirping delightedly in getting this semi-permission to do a semi-unconventional thing—- getting into a compartment before it is even part of the train! Then again, who is conventional in emergencies!

It was hard to push away from the ticket window as I was practically pinned to it by the eager arms flailing forward with the price of a ticket to Gola Gokaranath where the big Mela (a religious festival) was in progress. Funny, this was the rush and crush we had all come early to avoid!

The hundred yards from the ticket window to the end of the platform, the drop down to the level of the tracks and across rows of naked rails to the lone-standing rail carriage, was a veritable obstacle course. Not only did I have to look up for a way through the sea of moving bodies, but down, to prevent stepping on the unmoving ones—-those late sleepers who had stretched out on the station platform for the night. To the unaccustomed eye it would resemble a disaster area; bodies entirely covered with tautly drawn cloths. The area under the sheets assured the sleeping ones their only privacy from the world of people and the ever-present pariah dogs and monkeys on the snoop for a stray morsel of food.

I tripped and picked myself up from an awkward sprawl over a signal cable running close to a track.. But it was no trouble locating the carriage in the early half light of dawn. Juggling my purse, pillow, and water jug, I pulled myself up the laddered steps and pushed open the door. The carriage wasn't lit since it was not yet attached to the train, but I was accustomed to the general layout of third class compartments. I felt my way to the middle section where two benches faced each other, sharing an open window.

It was a relief to sit down on the smoothly worn slat bench after such a scramble. Although still quite dark, I looked out across the tracks to the movement on the lighted platform. At least I could sit in comfort for a while. This piece of train would soon get shoved back and forth until its bumpers would clank against the bumpers of the last car of the main train and lock in place—I hoped!

I sighed at the thought of the four children back in the mission house and wondered if they had gone back to bed and slept—or was there a pillow wet with tears after saying goodbye to mama? Could Dan keep the younger ones away from the well? Would Esther pester Dan as usual? Oh, I hope Jethi Ayah wouldn't put sugar in Beth's milk at breakfast—she hated that, and I had forgotten to remind her. I hoped, too, that Joey would push the screen doors shut after toddling in and out ... not as easy as supposed since the recent rains had swollen the frames. The fly and frog population INSIDE the house always increased under these circumstances.

"Oh, quit worrying," I told myself, and promptly turned the worry knob to another channel. "Wish Sam was here. Husbands are always away when emergencies happen!"

Sam was in Central India in meetings and didn't even know about the letter I had received from the Indian Government to appear in court for illegally importing American currency into the country. They had evidence and I was given the chance to appear and explain myself or be fined and imprisoned. I relived for the hundredth time the shock experienced when the letter had come. I began thinking about what I would say to the judge.

"Sir, I didn't intentionally break the law by importing foreign money. It had been my birthday and my friend in America sent it as a birthday present.... Yes, I know that in India we GIVE gifts on our birthdays instead of RECEIVING them, but the customs in America are backwards!.... Yes, I know that I can't spend a dollar in India, but I would have taken it to a bank to exchange for Rupees, and then I could have made a statement where it came from...."

On and on I planned rebuttals in my defense for I surely did not want to be fined Rs. 3000/— or spend six months in jail,—or both! Instinctively my heart cried out, "Oh, dear God, I need Your help, NOW. You've scooped me out of jams before. I don't know how You'll do it, Lord, but I am trusting You! Amen."

The wireless operator on the platform began the prestigious task of banging the piece of hanging rail with a hammer, announcing to the world that the train had left the last station and would soon be pulling into Lakhimpur. The crisp ding-ding-ding died out and with it the last vestige of calm on the platform. Mothers with bundles on their heads grabbed little ones onto their hips and yelled to bigger ones out of reach to stay close. Fathers with little ones straddling their shoulders and carrying their trusty "Dundas" (Solid 7 foot walking sticks) yelled to the mothers not to lag. Dogs scattered between the myriad feet, yelping when they got in the way. Vendors selling tea, sweets, peanuts, or chili-hot gram and "biris " (paperless cigarettes) raised their voices even louder.

"Single Daun!" the cry arose—an English corruption of "The signal is down!" That, in India, means the train is free to come in. I peered out my window and saw the bright eye of the engine and heard the steam pushing from it as the train approached. Soon it had passed me pulling its compartments full of human cargo. It shisshed to a halt by the platform. For a few moments I relished my solitude which I knew couldn't last much longer. Sure enough, the shunting engine bumped my reverie and started our series of back and forth movement until we joined the train at the platform.

It never fails to amuse and amaze me how everybody at one end of the platform has to rush and push to the other end while those at the far end find it necessary to jostle their noisy way to the opposite end of the train. Could it be the old nature in all of us which feels "Far off fields look greener," or that "compartments at the other end of the train look emptier?"

Rush, pull, push, yell they did in every direction, trying to get even one leg into the train somehow!

Would-be travelers attempted to mash their meager bundles in through the windows then tried to follow their goods. The compartment doors stood open with countless human wedges. I was standing claim to the seat by my window viewing the chaos and secretly chuckling over my early morning maneuver—at least I would have air to breathe when the mob pressed in!

Whether it was gradual or sudden awareness, I can't recall, but panic grabbed me when I realized that everybody was by-passing my compartment after looking in the window. I began to think there must be something grossly wrong with it and called to the guard as he went by.

"Guard Sahib, what's wrong with this compartment?"

He took the whistle out of his mouth, adjusted his pith helmet, and looked at the compartment, then at me. "Madam, I cannot help it that the whole train is so full. You should not be on safari at mela time." He shrugged his shoulders and went off leaving me none the wiser.

What people were saying as they peered into my compartment before rushing on, puzzled me even more. In short, they all expressed the same definite view, "BHARA PARA HAI" —(It is stuffed to capacity!)

A man tried to push his wife and child through the door not ten empty feet from me. She wasn't making any headway so he pushed her aside and tried with one leg to crawl over some enormous obstacle—which, for the life of me, I could not see. In moments he gave up, shoved her backwards out the door onto the platform muttering, "Bekar," —(It's useless!)

The guard blew his whistle and last minute

scrambling took place all over the station as the old train strained its slow start down the track. I looked out the window and was amazed to see so many people hanging on all over the outside, even on the roof, The train was truly "BHARA,"— that is , all except my compartment!

The door began banging back and forth as the train gained momentum. It was best to get up and shut it. Actually, I wanted to see why that man couldn't get in!

I had no trouble walking to the door for there was nothing in the way! Puzzled, I bolted the door. Still standing and swaying with the motion of the train, it began to dawn on me—I can feel again the grin of surprise and realization, and "dumbfoundedness bewilderment," all mixed together with peace.

"God, You did it! You've sent Your angels to fill this place! That's what I read to the children last night... "He will give His angels charge over thee, to keep thee in all thy ways." I wasn't praying that for me, Lord, but for the kids. You included me! How great! Thank You, Lord."

I was on Holy ground...even if it was rolling. I sat down. The wooden bench was a throne. The dirty floor didn't look so bad. If angels were sharing it with me, why should I complain? Such special company! And the journey had only begun!

I audibly thanked the Lord who had sent His Angels. I figured their job was done. Was I ever wrong!!!

— Chapter 13 —

The Odyssey Continues

The train clacked along in the early morning freshness. An eiderdown of haze hung low over the little patches of wheat and rye fields. The closely set mud villages with their blackened thatch roofs looked pretty, even with their walls speckled with cow dung patties put there for the sun to dry into fuel for cooking fires. Sleepy boys began herding water buffaloes towards jungle foraging.

There were bathers at the village wells. Indian men are meticulous whenever or wherever morning finds them, sloshing freshly drawn well water over their gleaming brown bodies in summer or in coldest winter. Even at railway stations, the platform pump is the most sought out spot during train stops! It's always intriguing to watch the clever dropping of the wet dhoti (yardage which makes into an Indian's trousers) and winding on the dry one in the same quick-trick technique of a practiced magician! I'm sure if I tried it, the result would be disastrous!

My "miracle" was duplicated at each station. Between stops I began to think of the times when angels had visited men in ancient times. There was no record that Daniel had seen the angels that muzzled the beasts, but they were there! Oh , yes, I remembered about poor Elisha's servant who was terribly frightened because the enemy had surrounded them on the top of a mountain and cried out to Elisha that this was surely their death! Then calm Elisha prayed and asked God to open the young man's eyes. For a moment God pulled back the curtain from his human eyesight and let him see the countless angels ready to defend them. Still, the very human in me kept expecting there might be a "changing of the guard" at each stop, or something.

Change, it did. The station after Gola where the train disgorged its tremendous load, I settled down on the worn bench breathing a "Thank You, God," in gratitude for the invisible companions I surely had had. I reached into the zippered pillowcase for my *Readers Digest*. I wanted to look officious if some men passengers got in. It just isn't the thing for a woman to travel unescorted.

The brakes squealed as the train halted. I took another look at the chain hanging above my head with its little red sign written in Hindi, Urdu, and English:.
"TO STOP TRAIN PULL CHAIN.
PENALTY FOR MISUSE RS. 50/-"

Again that human in me noted, if not audibly, "Well, that's close if I need it!" Oh me of little faith!

The door flew open and a corpulent Brahman gentleman entered. His servant rushed in and laid out a gadda (a thin cotton mattress) for him to sit on, then left. With the whole compartment at his disposal, I wondered with dismay why he had to choose the bench directly opposite mine, with our knees practically bumping. I made no move. After all, I was there first! Two minutes later his servant reappeared and proceeded to open a bundle and spread before him a sumptuous meal. Again, he disappeared only to rush back with a lota (a spouted metal vessel) of fresh water, and off just in time to hang on the outside of the train as we gained speed.

My heart bumped at the latest development, and I mentally practiced the 'To Stop Train Pull Chain' bit above and behind me, and kept "reading" my *Digest*. The aroma of his fresh purathas (delicious fried bread) called up a tremendous response in my own hungry anatomy. Every minute was torture. At the next stop I would order some tea and toast—a pretty safe thing since any germs would come boiled or toasted.

The man took no notice of me, nor attempted conversation. Neither did I speak. It was impossible to understand why he ate his food with me so very close to it—an act not done by a man of his high caste. This would be sure defilement of his food and person. His loud belch announced complete satisfaction and brought me up sharp. I wondered, 'what now?' and returned to my "reading." Actually, I don't recall turning any pages.

As soon as the train stopped, I put my head out the window and waved to the vendor and called, "Behra, mujhko chai tos chaiye," (Waiter, I would like some tea and toast), relieved at contact with another person. The waiter handed me the tray with a steaming pot of tea and two small squares of toast and butter through the window. I propped myself against the back of the bench and put the small pillow on my lap to balance the tray. As I stirred the leaves around in the pot I thought, "If he didn't object to my proximity when he ate, why should I worry about endangering his caste!" I sprinkled some sugar on the toast and sipped the good tea while the train continued to carry me towards Delhi.

No conversation passed between us. My companion stretched out on his bench and breathed heavily.

But the screeching brakes at the next station interrupted his comfy repose. The tea vendor came into the compartment to claim his tray and I asked, "How much do I owe you?"

"Seventy-five naiya paisa," came the reply.

I put the money on the tray and handed it to the waiter over the reclining man, who, at that very instant, sat bolt upright and knocked the tray with his head sending the pot, cup saucer, sugar, and money in clattering crashes to the floor.

He turned and saw the waiter and gruffly demanded, "Kya karte ho? (What are you doing?), I did not order any tea!"

"I know, Maharaj. I was just getting the tray from memsahib," defended the waiter as he picked up the scattered pieces and left the compartment something less than happy!

Obviously seeing and hearing me for the first time, he rearranged his clothes, gathered his legs under him, and with puzzlement oozing from his expression, demanded in very polite Hindi, "When did you get in?"

The truth flashed in my brain. How quickly the mind computes. I knew instantly why he had eaten so freely in my presence, and lounged so unconcernedly! HE REALLY HAD NOT SEEN ME UNTIL THIS MOMENT!

"Sir, I have been on this bench since Lakhimpur station this morning," I replied with false complacency.

This answer baffled him. The wheels of perplexity began spinning in his head when he suddenly grabbed his gadda and dishes and made for the door. The last I heard he was muttering loudly, "Hey Ram, Ram!" (Oh God, God!).

I didn't feel exactly strong myself—and more than a little foolish by my own obvious lack of understanding. If God could fill my compartment with angelic passengers for my protection at one time, why couldn't He just as easily make this same compartment look EMPTY when I needed THAT? And I had glibly assured the ticket man I was prepared for ANYTHING! God must have a sense of humor!

The business in the court at Delhi was anticlimactic. Surely, I was delighted and relieved when His Honor, a kindly judge, reprimanded me for the horrendous error of bringing undeclared foreign currency into the country. He was, indeed, considerate and dismissed the charges on my promise to enlighten my faulty friends who send money in envelopes. I headed for Lakhimpur the next morning.

No sooner had I reached home and given out the promised presents from Delhi (a bar of Cadbury's chocolate for each), when Jethi informed me that the children had been quite cooperative—a somewhat loaded statement which I could interpret any way I wanted!

"And memsahib, every time they started to run towards the well, they stopped and ran back."

Amazing!

"And what did you all learn while Mama was gone?" I queried, to reinforce a rule in our house that each of us should learn something new each day.

Between munches of almond chocolate, Dan informed me he learned why Daddy called Barre, our German shepherd, a male dog.

With trepidation I responded, "Oh yes?"—not, "Why?"

Retrieving a chocolate crumb from his shoe, he

announced anyway, "He tried to bite the mail man!"

Esther disappeared momentarily and rushed back displaying a little contraption, "This is my tarazu (scales). I made it with two sides of a Kiwi tin, (shoe polish tin), and a stick and some string. All the safety pins and bobby pins in your drawer weigh eight marbles. I didn't get much polish on my hands 'cause I cleaned the tins out first with my towel," she added thoughtfully to reassure me.

"Oh, that's great!" I managed in admiration and agony.

Not to be outdone, Beth declared she had found out where a big, big, snake lived—"Right by the well. Joe and I saw him there two days so we didn't go there after that."

Joe, up on my hip, spread his own two chubby arms as far as they could stretch and with big round eyes, confirmed, "B A R A samp" (BIG snake).

My heart somersaulted, not only because of the thought of a snake near the children, but the very unlikelihood of a big snake being in the same spot twice, especially when the well is used so constantly by so many on the compound. God certainly has His ways of taking care of His children!

Dan announced another discovery. "Mama, Esther and I found out why we are Americans."

"Really? Why?" I asked. He licked his fingers and quickly withdrew four different American coins from his pocket, and simultaneously plunked himself down on the cement floor with motions for us all to do the same. On following suit, my immediate reaction was...Aw,Aw, they've been into my coin collection...then, horrors,— undeclared American currency!

He was turning the coins over and pointing, "See?"

"See what?" I squinted.

"Look, Mom, it says 'IN GOD WE TRUST'."

The Beckdahl Family

Ruth dispensing love, prayer and sore throat medicines to boys in our Mission School in Newabganj, Gonda.

Ruth loved people, God's promises and plants.

In honour of
Her Majesty, Queen Elizabeth II
and
His Royal Highness, The Prince Philip, Duke of Edinburgh

The Commonwealth High Commissioners in India
request the pleasure of the company of

Rev. & Mrs. S. Beckdale,

at a Reception on Wednesday, 25th January, 1961
from 12 noon to 1.0 p.m.
at 2, King George's Avenue, New Delhi.

R.S.V.P.
The Comptroller to the
U.K. High Commissioner
2, King George's Avenue
New Delhi. 2.

Lounge Suit or
National Dress

Actual invitation received to have tea with Queen Elizabeth and Prince Phillip.

Ruth decorated the entire gym walls when teaching about the first Americans.

Ruth's farewell banquet when she retired from teaching.

Springfield Education Association

extends to

Ruth Beckdahl

upon retirement, recognition and gratitude for faithful services as a member of the instructional staff of

Springfield Public Schools

and as a contributor during many years to the purposes and achievements of public education.

Dear Mrs. Beckdahl,
 I think your the nices and sweetest person I know. I Love you! Love
        Sarah Powell

Dear Mrs. Beckdahl,
 I Love you more than anything in the hole wide world. Thank you for everything you have done for me,
  ♡ ♡ ♡ Love Richard   ♡ ♡ ♡
        Good bye

Teacher's Prayer

I want to teach my students how
        To live this life on earth
To face its struggles and its strife
        And improve their worth
Not just the lesson in a book
        Or how the rivers flow
But how to choose the proper path
        Wherever they may go
To understand eternal truth
        And know the right from wrong
And gather all the beauty of
        A flower and a song
For if I help the world to grow
        In wisdom and in grace
Then I shall feel that I have won
        And I have filled my place
And so I ask your guidance, God
        That I may do my part
For character and confidence
        And happiness of heart.
            James J. Metcalf

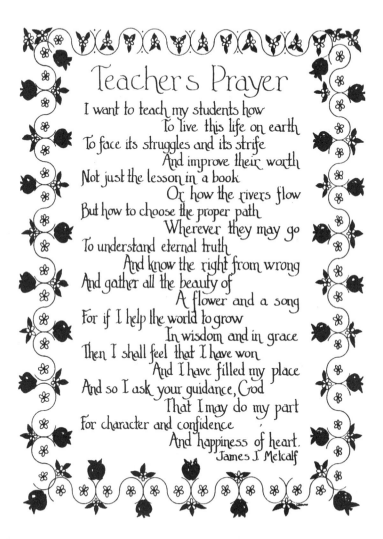

Masai shield and neck ornament from East Africa

Kiambogo- the main building at the school. Taken the day we took the children back to school. The name means "Rhinoceros." "Buffalo"

CERTIFICATE OF SPECIAL RECOGNITION

This certifies that

MRS BECKDAHL

is Awarded this
Certificate of Special Recognition for

"to a special teacher that made a difference to the class of 1988"

Given at Hillcrest High School   May , 19 88

Principal

SR Class Pres.

— Chapter 14 —

"And Solomon Awoke and Lo, It Was a Dream"
I Kings 3:15

God allowed King Solomon to dream a wonderful dream telling him what would come to pass if he adhered to God's Law. And it did.

Joseph had two unusual dreams and he told his brothers about them. They became angry and jealous of him and sold him into slavery. That didn't stop his dreams from becoming reality later in his life.

Joseph, husband of Jesus' mother had a God sent dream. When he awoke he obeyed what God had showed him to do—to flee with Mary and Jesus into Egypt.

Throughout the Bible there are lots of instances where God sent dreams and visions to His people. Now I am not putting myself on a par with these people of old, but I have had some wonderful dreams that have "come to pass".

One such dream started when I was very young: Being in India back then, we were surrounded with all things British. "Punch and Judy" puppet shows, or their comics, "High Tea," in proper attire, and the clipped accents of the British military. The singing of "God Save the King," was present at every social function.

We loved the Royal Family and followed their

news constantly. Princesses Elizabeth and Margaret were not much younger than I was so it was always of interest to me to hear about them as they became teenagers. Oh, the excitement when Princess Elizabeth met Phillip and they fell in love!

We kept our ears to the static of the radio and strained to hear about the Princess's trip to Kenya where she visited and stayed at the famed "Tree Tops" hotel built literally in the trees. Elephants and zebra and antelope roamed around under them on the forest floor, while their majesties gazed in awe. Not a detail escaped my curious and interested mind. Then the blow struck. A cable (telegram) came from London to the Princess stating, "Your father, the King, has succumbed to lung cancer today. You will now assume the duties of the Queen of England and the British Isles. Long live the Queen".

Fortunately, her fiancé Phillip Mountbatton was with her. What a heavy message for the young Princess. She knew that she had to be strong. I lived through it all with her and prayed for her fortitude. The Royal party left immediately for Britain.

There followed news of the transition of the monarchy to the new "Queen" Elizabeth. She and "Prince" Phillip, as he became at their marriage, made a handsome couple. I listened with keen interest as their family grew and experienced many different avenues of Service to their country and adoring public.

I grew up also and went to college in America before returning to India to be married. My own husband, Samuel Beckdahl, was a Britisher, not an Englishman, but a Britisher, by virtue of being born in India and serving in the British/Indian Army. I had dual nationality by being born in India to American citizens. I chose to be an American at age eighteen. Then when I married Sam, once again British citizenship was conferred on me. Now that I lived in India and British circles once again, the Royal Family reoccupied my thoughts.

Our family grew in size and age. Queen Elizabeth and Prince Phillip had four children as we did. They did many of the things we enjoyed doing, picnicking, hunting, and traveling. It didn't seem strange at all to me that I resumed dreaming about their family. Almost every night my dreams included visits with them. We became friends and often went on trips together. We had camping gear they often borrowed. Sam and Prince Phillip often hunted together as Sam knew the best places to go. We knew what they liked to eat and play.

In reality, every morning at breakfast Sam asked me about my latest dream and I would relate every detail to him. The children often asked, "Where did you go last night, Mommie? Balmoral Castle?" Sam thought it was funny. I now wish I had taped these answers as I told him what I had experienced each night. Our family went on furlough for a year to the United States and then we returned to India for another term. My dreams continued all along.

One day, back in India, the postman brought us a surprise. It was an invitation from the British High Commissioner in Delhi to come and have "Tea with Her Majesty Queen Elizabeth and Prince Phillip." This was no dream! My joy knew no bounds, after all, I knew them as "old friends"!

The two weeks dragged until our trip to Delhi. On arrival we found the place, a large parade ground set with guide ropes and red carpet. Many others had also been invited. My anticipation grew as we saw the Royal Couple step onto the carpet and slowly come closer. They were accompanied by several other people, including the British High Commissioner and his wife. I pressed against the rope in a surge of joy. Here was my dream coming true. What's more, when their Majesties came down the lane they stopped in front of Sam and me! We actually talked! She was so beautiful and so real. I told her I felt like I knew them well because I had dreamed nightly about them and their family. I told her that I had prayed much for them since the death of her father, King George VI. She expressed appreciation and said with her white gloved hand holding mine, "Please, don't stop now!"

Sam had a few words with Prince Phillip before they moved on. I don't remember what we ate or drank at "Tea." My heart was singing. I never dreamed about them again. My heart was somehow satisfied. I have continued to pray for Her Majesty, as she requested.

Now I am looking forward with great anticipation and joy for when the clouds will part and the "King of Kings" will come in glory to gather His children. Oh what joy that will be! It is not just a dream but a reality! It will happen. He has promised!

— Chapter 15 —

Dr. Jesus Will See You Now

It was the middle of June during the 10 day school break. Sam had come up to the mountains to take the family with him to the Kulu Valley, another mountainous area in north India. The McDearmid family was with us in their own station wagon. We drove through the heat of the day on the plains and were approaching Ludhiana, with the others well in the lead. We found this to be a good way to travel because of the dust our vehicles kicked up.

Suddenly a cow started to cross the road and stopped right in front of us. Our brakes squealed and Sam swerved to miss the animal. It is surprising how fast your brain works at times like that! At that time it was a very serious offense to hit a cow in India, even more serious than hitting a person.

In swerving so sharply our vehicle rolled over several times and went down the steep embankment, coming to rest on its wheels and the engine still running. Thank God for the ledge that stopped us from rolling farther. The contents of our car was scattered and the roof pushed in and the windshield was smashed but none of us was seriously hurt. Praising God, we got out to check us all over. Only the top of my head felt numb from the severe bump. We gathered our gear and the potatoes that had been scattered around and contemplated our next move.

After an hour, the McDearmids missed us and

came back to find curious onlookers gazing over the side of the road. We were so grateful for the McDearmids' help and that of the crowd who pulled and pushed to get the car back up the slope and onto the road. The cow was safe and sound!

We continued our journey to Kulu although the car looked as though it had been through the war. We camped by the stream and the children had fun. On our open fire we contrived an oven using two pans and Bernice made a cherry pie! That was the only place in India that I ever saw cherries! Was that ever good!

Too soon the children's vacation was over and we uncovered the car from its protective tarp and "dents and all" drove back up to Mussoorie. It took nine months before the replacement windshield arrived from the States and about six months to get all the dents pounded out!

After reaching home I started experiencing head aches and neck pains. We prayed much but couldn't understand why no relief came. Three months passed and when I couldn't bear the pain any more we sought out a missionary doctor who was an orthopedic surgeon. After x-rays, surgery was performed and he found, besides the two crushed vertebrae, a large blood tumor was forming made up of hundreds of blood vessels that filled with each pulsation of my heart and caused me excruciating pain. After the six hour surgery I was put in a body cast from the top of my head to my hips. Only my face, arms and legs were free. Sand bags were placed in my bed to prevent any movement at all.

As soon as I opened my eyes I realized something else was amiss. I had triple vision that didn't go away even after days in hospital. I saw three doctors, three nurses, three husbands! I knew I only had one, Sam! My doctor was very concerned. I cried out to God, "Oh Lord, have mercy on me. I have four children, a husband and lots of work to do. Please, help me!"

The next morning my doctor came in with another doctor and after introducing us, said, "My friend is from Switzerland where he is an eye specialist. He has been visiting me and I would like for him to examine your eyes if that would be okay with you."

"Sure," I said. "That would be great."

His examination proceeded and he said he would like to consider the matter until the next day.

I told him that I wasn't going anywhere and I'd be there!

The next day when the two doctors came in, he explained he had a patient in Switzerland with the same problem. He had made her a pair of prism-glasses that had proved helpful in eliminating the triple vision. She had been using them for the past two and a half years but complained of their bulkiness.

Again my heart cried out to God, "You are Jehovah Rapha, the God that healeth and my trust is in You, Lord."

The doctor said he would be in the next morning to take exact measurements so he could make the prism glasses for me.

True to his word he arrived with my doctor and started to set up his instruments. That is when it occurred. He said, "Look at me." I looked and immediately realized that I saw only one of him!

I looked toward my doctor and again saw only one of him! Back and forth I glanced and excitedly told them my eyes were okay! It took a few minutes to prove and reiterate that something had indeed taken place and my vision was really corrected.

The kind doctors rejoiced with me. My doctor was quick to say, "We have a Higher Power at work here!"

"This is a miracle!" the Swiss Doctor exclaimed. I excitedly agreed and told them of my faith.

The next week Sam took me, cast and all, up to our mission cottage, called Claremont, in the mountains of Mussoorie. I traveled on a mattress in the back of our station wagon. The heat on the plains was severe, especially in a large cast.

We took the kids out of boarding and Sam took Dan, Beth, and Joe and went on a campout. While they were gone, Jheti Ayah and Esther stayed with me to tend to my needs. Jheti was too scared to help, but Esther and I took paring and butcher knives to cut the cast off. I had had enough of the "coffin-feeling" to last a lifetime! Between the two of them I was able to get up and learn to walk again.

Postscript to this story...

It was furlough time six months after that. We found ourselves back in the States and once again in the groove of visiting churches that had supported us while we were overseas engaged in Missionary work.

Sam and I were visiting the Stone Church in Chicago where our friend Mrs. Nicodem attended, and were asked to join the pastor on the platform Sunday morning. The Pastor introduced us. While greeting the church body a lady in the congregation waved her hand vigorously to get our attention. "I recognize you, Sister Ruth, though we have never met." She continued, "The Lord woke me up one night some months ago and gave me a vision of your face, and said, "Get up and pray for Ruth's eyes. She is in India!" I never knew your last name but I was sure God directed me to pray for you. I got up beside my bed and prayed, then got back into bed and fell asleep."

Later we ascertained that it was the very time the Swiss doctor came into my hospital room in Ludhiana Hospital in India to take the measurements for prism glasses. Midnight in the central USA was the late morning in India! God does hear our cries!! And He honors our faith. How kind of Him to awaken someone who was willing to intercede for someone she did not even know!

Since then, I have had perfect eyesight. At age eighty I can thread a needle and read all the street names for my husband as we travel. "The rest of the story?" as Paul Harvey says....When I went to get my driver's license renewed a few months back, the examiner asked, "Where are your glasses?"

My reply was, "I don't wear glasses."

"Then do you have your contacts in your eyes?"

"God healed my eyes many years ago." I answered.

"Lets see!" he said as he put me through the eye testing machine.

"Perfect score! Beats all I ever heard!" he remarked.

I grinned and pointed upward.

— Chapter 16 —

Uhuru!
Psalm 91

*He that dwelleth in the secret place of the most High
shall abide under the shadow of the Almighty
I will say of the Lord, He is my refuge and my fortress:
my God; in him will I trust.
Surely he shall deliver thee from the snare of the fowler,
and from the noisome pestilence.
He shall cover thee with his feathers,
and under his wings shalt thou trust:
his truth shalt be thy shield and buckler.
Thou shalt not be afraid for the terror by night;
nor for the arrow that flieth by day;
Nor for the pestilence that walketh in darkness;
nor for the destruction that wasteth at noonday.
A thousand shall fall at thy side
and ten thousand at thy right hand;
but it shall not come nigh thee.
Only with thine eyes shalt thou behold
and see the reward of the wicked.
Because thou hast made the Lord, which is my refuge,
even the most High, thy habitation;
There shall no evil befall thee,
neither shall any plague come near thy dwelling.
For he shall give his angels charge over thee,
to keep thee in all thy ways.
They shall bear thee up on their hands,*

lest thou dash thy foot against a stone.
Thou shalt tread upon the lion and the adder:
the young lion and the dragon shalt thou trample under thy feet.
Because he has set his love upon me,
therefore will I deliver him:
I will set him on high, because he hath known my name.
He shall call upon me, and I will answer him:
I will be with him in trouble;
I will deliver him, and honor him.
With long life will I satisfy him,
and shew him my salvation.

AFRICA!

This was a whole new mission field for us. Naturally it was different in many ways, yet it held many similarities. We went to Tanganyika knowing we would be ministering to the large East Indian population located in the coastal capital city, Dar es Salaam. Many, many skilled, highly trained and educated, lawyers, doctors, and businessmen and women had left their native land and immigrated to Tanganyika and Kenya for greater vocational opportunities. So we would no longer be nearly so involved with the rural population as we had been in the villages of India. It was a whole new challenge and we welcomed it.

The children were attending Rift Valley Academy in Kenya and we felt at the time, that all would be well. The work was progressing slowly in the store front we had rented and turned into a reading room and Church hall in the city. People were coming to know the Savior. Relationships were being built, and friendships forged.

While we were there in the early sixties there

was a period of great political unrest in all of East Africa, and a revolution, instigated by the Chinese Communists. During those awful days the majority of the Arab population on Zanzibar were massacred or expelled. The country became Tanzania as a result of the political union between mainland Tanganyika and the offshore islands of Zanzibar and Pemba. That said, the Indian population we had come to serve were being slaughtered or leaving in droves, having to abandon everything that they had. All Americans, Europeans, and the British were unsafe. The shouts of "Uhuru" (Freedom) swelled everywhere. What it really meant was anarchy! The American consulate had warned us to be ready to leave at any moment, to have escape plans ready, and supplies for basic survival. We heard on London's BBC that one of our own missionaries, Brother Joseph Tucker had been murdered in the Congo by the "Simba." He had been bludgeoned to death and thrown to the crocodiles while his children were forced to watch!

    That morning while Sam and I were having our devotions we were reading the 91st Psalm. In such a time of anxiety it was pure balm to our souls! As we prayed, we were both impressed to leave immediately and go to Kenya! It was not something we could argue with, we KNEW we must! We immediately got in the car and headed over to the Friesen's house to let them know what we were doing and to ask if Norm Correll wanted to come with us, knowing that he had been stranded in Dar without any word on his family up north. All communication had been cut off for days. We had been under home confinement and it was a very scary time.

Norm was out on the porch when we arrived, and without even turning off the motor Sam asked if he wanted to go home. He quickly grabbed his stuff and came with us and told us he had been expecting us! He had been having his devotions that morning, reading Psalm 91, and the Lord had let him know he was to go home right away and to be ready to leave when we came! We had no way of notifying him! Asked if he had heard an audible voice tell him, he said, "No, it was more definite than that!"

Since we could not use the roads in and around the city, Norm asked if Sam knew any way of getting up to the main road going north without encountering the rebels? Sure enough, he did, and we drove off through the maize fields and banana plantations until we were able to get to the road.

We were stopped several times by soldiers in camouflage, bushes and leaves used as headdress. They did us no harm and let us pass.

As we approached the junction to Arusha, near where Norm and Norma lived we saw a car parked beside the road up ahead. As we got close, Norm recognized it as their car! Norma and Brian, their young son, were waiting by the road for us! During devotions that morning, Norma had been reading the 91st Psalm and she had been told by the Lord to be there, at that time, because we were coming!

God used His Word and His Spirit to impress each of us so miraculously, and had placed His guardian angels around our car and had kept us safe. From there we went many miles further north and finally reached mountainous Kijabe to collect our children. What a relief to hold them close. Each mile had been a miracle.

God wonderfully protected us as we turned and sped back south to Dar es Salaam. The unrest eventually simmered down a bit. We remained vigilant. It was much better having the children where we knew how it was for them. We were alert to the white slavery trade that was known to exist on the coast but we did enjoy the beautiful white sand beaches occasionally and spent some quality time there with the kids and our friends as an outlet.

Esther had developed chronic malaria, a debilitating illness and we decided it would be good for her to return to the States and my folks had graciously said they would let her live with them. We made a family vacation out of driving down to South Africa to put her on the plane. It was a relief to do something fun and we knew she would be in good hands. It would be a year before we saw her again. By then, my own health was in terrible shape and we came back to the States, also. The work we had begun in Dar es Salaam was turned over to a new and lovely elderly missionary couple.God blessed them there. Uhuru! Freedom has many meanings. I am glad that mine is found in Him!

— Chapter 17 —

Bonnie and Clyde
(Stateside)

In second grade little boys are very sweet but they don't always think before they act. Hank and Sherman rushed into my classroom in Robberson School one morning each carrying a baby bird in their cupped hands. "Mrs. Beckdahl, Mrs. Beckdahl, here are some baby birds for you! We know how much you love animals so we brought them so you could look after them." On inquiring where they got them, I learned they had shot the mother bird with a "BB" gun the evening before. They didn't have a clue how to care for the babies who were apparently only a few days old, and Hank's mother told them to get rid of them. They couldn't bear to "get rid of them" so decided the best course of action was to bring them to their teacher and get her to look after them.

I didn't have any idea what kind of birds they were. My heart went out to them hearing their doleful "cheep, cheep, cheeping." Their eyes were not even open yet. I suspected they were pigeons. I had never observed what baby pigeons eat but obviously the tiny creatures were hungry. We got some cotton and soaked it in water to squeeze a little moisture into their beaks. My woolen gloves formed a "nest" and they quieted down temporarily. Of course the class got in on the act. We discussed what we could feed them. Wonderful suggestions were forthcoming—worms, fruit, apple seeds, milk, bread, cheese, seeds, etc, etc. We discussed the sadness of the death of the mother who couldn't look after them now. During all our learning of Math, Spelling, Reading, and Writing many wise deductions about the plight of motherless creatures were offered by the children and valuable lessons were learned.

The children brought bits of their lunches hidden in napkins and tried coaxing our wee orphans who didn't know how to eat any of their offerings. Finally school was out and I was left with my little featherless babies to take home and be their surrogate mama.

I dug worms. No deal. They weren't interested. I found little bugs and tried to put them in their wide open beaks. They nearly choked. Finally I ground up some raw oatmeal and moistened it and put tiny pellets in their mouths. Voila! They ate it and survived. I added cream of wheat and sometimes corn meal. It worked!

Gradually my little charges grew feathers and began strutting around. They thought I was their mother and I felt like it too because I got very attached to my "Bonnie" and "Clyde." They did turn out to be pigeons all right and trailed behind me everywhere I went. I loved it. They had a box on our screened back porch, but they'd sneak in the door if it didn't get closed quickly enough! Feeding them was easy now and they loved bird seed and almost everything I offered them.

One day when I didn't close the door fast enough, Clyde got part way in when the door closed on his leg and broke it. I was horrified and made a little match stick splint for him taped with strips of band aid. He hobbled around for quite a spell but finally recovered with a small bend in his leg. Strangely enough some feathers started to grow straight out where the break had occurred. He had a limp but it didn't stop him from flying and walking around with Bonnie and following me, his "Mama" wherever he could. Whenever I would come home from school, they would fly up on my shoulders or my head and even accepted my husband as part of our "family".

It was the beginning of summer and we had just bought a house about five miles out in the country. With five acres of beautiful oak trees and plenty of garden space, Bonnie and Clyde loved it too. I had a nice "house" for them on the back deck. They took to it immediately. I had a Guernsey cow named "Daisy Mae" who would stand beneath our bedroom window and call me by mooing at five in the morning to come and milk her. As soon as I'd get dressed and head down to the barn where she was waiting, my birds would fly down and sit on my shoulder while I milked her. They made friends with Daisy Mae too. Our dog Lassie would allow me to put Bonnie and Clyde on her back.

One of the most fun things was when we would have a picnic on our deck with some friends from Central Bible College. Bonnie and Clyde would swoop down and land on someone's head or shoulder and expect a piece of bread or bun. Of course we wouldn't warn them! It was fun to hear their shrieks or see them spill their lemonade!

School started again in the Fall and I had my class on the playground as we were learning about rocks and their composition. Pointing to one particular rock with my right foot left me with my weight on my left leg when a hard thrown soft ball came from behind and hit me in the back of my knee. Down I went, turning slamming into the ground, I knew something broke inside. My knee required immediate care and surgery in Cox Medical Center in Springfield.

I lay there in traction for days. A young neighbor came to our place to milk Daisy Mae. I missed her morning "mooing" so much. I missed my Bonnie and Clyde too! One day when the nurse was taking my "vitals," I gazed out the 3rd floor window of my room and there were Bonnie and Clyde pecking at the glass. I got rid of the thermometer and excitedly told the nurse that those were my pigeons and they had found me!

"Oh yes," she said, "and that is my robin in the sky! How do you know that those are your pigeons?"

"Look at the leg on the big one. If you see two feathers growing out of the middle of its leg, that is my Clyde!" I declared. Out of curiosity she went over to look. "Sure enough!" she said in surprise. Too bad that the windows were sealed for the air-conditioning! But my little ones had found me in an unfamiliar place, my very room, from five miles out of town! I was overjoyed and praised God who had made those wonderful instincts in pigeons.

Now tell me, if birds can locate people with such accuracy, is it not easy for the God who planted that ability in the birds, to know just where His children are at any time? He has said:

"The eyes of the Lord run to and fro throughout the whole earth, to show Himself strong on the behalf of them whose hearts are perfect towards Him…" II Chron. 16:9

Jesus said, "I will never leave thee nor forsake thee." Hebrews 13:5

My Family

Daniel Frederick
Esther Elise
Elizabeth Anne
Joseph Christian
Samuel Thelle Beckdahl
Verne Ballard MacKinney

— Chapter 18 —
Daniel Frederick
"Oh, Danny Boy"

Psalm 127: 3-5
"Sons are a heritage from the Lord. Children are a reward from Him.
Like arrows in the hands of a warrior are the sons born in ones youth.
Blessed is the man whose quiver is full of them..."

One of the things I have learned in my sojourn on earth is the certainty of God's Word.

While I grew up I remember having a lot of pain in my abdomen and surrounding regions. As a young woman engaged to be married, I was living and working in New York City saving for my journey back to India during WWII. Several abdominal attacks within two months prompted my wise mother to say, "Sounds like appendicitis to me! Better have it checked out before leaving the States."

She was my medical guru. She had been an "OR nurse" for the then famous Dr. Walter Grey Crump before she went to India. He still did advisory cases but his son, Dr. W.G. Crump, Jr. was now becoming a famous New York surgeon in his own right. Mother said that I must go to see him. The appointment was made and I dutifully submitted to that awful examination of my innards. Sure enough, appendicitis was reaching the acute stage. Unbeknown to me, Mom had told him "on the side," of "problems" I had encountered since childhood. SO, "exploratory surgery" was performed while extricating the offending appendix. Recovery was speedy. The doctor was kind. He pulled up a chair and informed me of the good news and the bad. The good was that the surgery had gone well but I had wrestled the doctor and five nurses while under anesthesia! They had to have all six people to keep me on the table!

"Ether Jag," I believe they called it. Evidently, my early sports training had given me unbelievable strength.

The "bad" news was that I had "underdeveloped reproductive organs and an infantile womb," meaning, I probably would never be able to have children.

What a blow! This was news I had to share with my future husband! He took the news calmly and only said, "I was counting on us having a full football team!"

Sam was an only child and recalled many lonely vacations with elderly parents. I assured him these things were in God's hands. I fully believed that. Even though he raised his eyebrows, he did very lovingly add, "I'll have you, anyway."

A year and a half went by after we were married and I began to feel decidedly unwell every evening. We were living in Benares Cantonments and I did not know of any doctors so I did not see any. I did not feel badly at all in the morning hours so I reasoned it couldn't be "morning sickness" like pregnancies were purported to produce. Besides, I wasn't supposed to be able to get pregnant! Months passed and by now I knew that our first football player was on the way! From then on, we enjoyed it immensely and began praying for our Daniel-

Esther, not knowing which it would be. Sam was now "demobilized" in the USA. That means after his six years of military service, he was ushered back into civilian life. We arrived in Boston Harbor on Christmas Eve in a snow storm. I was seven months along now without having visited a "baby doctor." As soon as we got to Springfield, Missouri, my Aunt Lillian got me toDr. Johnson, her own daughter's obstetrician. He was wonderful. All was in order. The Lord had protected me even without any medical advice.

The day after Danny was born in St. Johns' Hospital, Dr. Johnson informed me he had never seen such an ecstatic father as Sam! He had given the Doctor a big bear hug! Sam was so proud of his son. At church he showed him off to everyone who would even glance in our direction! My joy and pride were unbounded and God had given us a 10 pound bouncer as the first arrow in our quiver. I remember holding him tight, walking up and down singing, "Oh, Danny Boy..." making up the rest of the words, "You are so beautiful, God gave us such a precious boy, the pipes, the pipes are calling.... You call and I must come..." Of course, every time the words changed and more joy poured out of our hearts as we gazed at our beautiful, bald, blue eyed, little giant, so strong from birth. Danny grew and increased in favor with God and us!

He grew so quickly and one day he toddled out the door. We hadn't noticed the eighteen-wheeler that had parked parallel to our trailer just outside our makeshift fence. Out the gate Dan went and stood behind the back wheel patting the tire with both his hands, his tummy pressed against the rubber. I glanced up just as the driver climbed in and started the engine.

If he backed up there was no way to save our little boy. The half second it took to call on God, He answered. The truck revved then slowly went forward causing Danny to fall on his face. While traumatic, that certainly was better than being crushed under that enormous wheel! Thank You, Lord!

At fifteen-and-a-half months Dan was joined by baby sister, Esther. He was an exceptionally good boy. He would do what we told him. I remember serving an Indian meal to a large group and didn't need him trailing me around. I picked him up and put him in an empty chair in the circle and said. "Stay here until I come and get you." He never moved, even when friends tried to coax him to come to them. He would take care of his sister when I requested that. He always looked at me when I talked to him, and did what I said.

From the beginning Dan showed great sensitivity to the moving of God. At three years of age he insisted on going down to the altar in the rural church Sam was pastoring. Dad had given an "altar call" and I could not keep Dan back thinking he did not understand. He wept as he knelt at the altar. I do believe he understood what Jesus had done for him on the cross.

Danny was decidedly left handed. No amount of coaxing would change that. When he entered Woodstock School in India his teachers commented on what a good boy he was. He always looked at them for directions and then did what he was told. Because of his obedience he was placed at the back of the room. He could be trusted to behave. He colored well, and "drew" very well, as long as he used his left hand. In that country no one was permitted to use their left hand. That was reserved for bathroom purposes. You could not give a gift with your left hand. You certainly could not eat with your left hand. No one could write left-handed or even gesture with it! Poor Dan! His teachers tried so hard to get him "straightened out." His right handed writing was unreadable. He read things backwards. "Saw" became "was," etc. He became more and more confused.

At a regular class medical screening, the nurse wrote us a note, "Daniel is very deaf. Please see to it."

I was stunned and decided to test him myself. Putting Dan and Esther at one end of the room I turned my back to them and in a normal voice asked them if they would like some candy. Esther shouted, "Sure!" and bounded towards me. Dan just stood there. I turned and repeated the question as he looked at me. "Yeah!" he responded. He had read my lips. My boy was deaf!

I arranged for an American missionary doctor to check Dan's hearing. He confirmed what we already knew. Dan was very deaf. He did suggest that removing his adenoids might help him to hear better. After the surgery the situation improved, but much damage had already been done. He was behind in almost all learning skills. He excelled in creative arts and sports. It is difficult not to cringe when I think that he had been placed at the back of the classroom because of his good behavior. It had made hearing even more difficult. This is a reminder to parents to have your children's hearing tested early.

I would not allow Esther to be promoted above him. He already hated that she could read better and they had to be in the same class. When I became an Elementary School Teacher later in life I realized that our boy was dyslexic. No wonder he read things backwards. Then he was born left-handed and not allowed to use his left hand. On top of that, he was very deaf. How I wish I had known all this earlier! By the 5th Grade, I put my foot down, and insisted that he be allowed to use his left hand. It was then he learned to write.

Dan was an avid adventurer. He loved the out of doors. One day when he was about seven years old he wanted to accompany his Dad and some preachers to the town of Gonda, about thirty miles away from where we were in Newabganj. Daddy had said, "No, we don't know when we will be getting back."

Dan had his own plan. He told Esther he was going to go anyway, and made her promise not to tell Mommy. As the Jeep station wagon started up, Danny jumped on the back bumper and held on to the handle and hinge. It was a terribly dangerous thing to have done. His head could not be seen in the rear view mirror because of the bundles in back. He just had to hang on for dear life.

Thirty miles isn't long on American good roads but on the oxcart furrowed road with constant jolts and bumps and six inch deep fine dust flaring up with every turn of the wheels, even inside the vehicle is not at all comfortable. I don't know how he was able to make it but believe it was by the grace of God!

I was beside myself after looking for Danny and finally being told what had happened. There was no vehicle on the premises I could chase them with. There were no phones or anyone to call for help! Sam would not even know if he fell off, because he didn't know that he was even there! My "wireless" to Heaven was in use right away. "Oh, God, please keep Your hand on Dan. Don't let him fall off or get killed. I am trusting You, Lord. Please send Your Guardian Angels on that Gonda

Road. Thank You, Lord! Amen."

I had to wait until evening to find out. The preachers told me that when they reached Gonda and got through the crowded bazaar, they stopped to buy a can of petrol. To their amazement, they saw this "Bhut" (apparition) standing by the back of the station wagon. This "thing" was completely covered with dust including the head, the eyelashes, ears and the whole body. Then it spoke and they recognized him as "Danny Baba." Sam in disbelief and shock paddled him on the spot, then hugged him, then brought him home less than pleased! What relief to me to see that little man!

As he grew, he had many adventures in the mountains with his little brother, Joey, out in the jungles with the family, even an eighty-four mile bicycle trek with one of our helpers to our friend's home in Lucknow, and then back.

We rode elephants. We camped and we hunted. He loved the many wild animals we saw in our travels.

In East Africa Dan was happy and very inventive. He was capable of taking apart and rebuilding just about anything. His most memorable project was the building of a motorcycle from parts gathered from junkyards and second hand shops. It turned out to be a 700 cc motorcycle. I was his assistant cutting gaskets and finding things to hock in order to buy bolts, nuts, and wires, anything for that cycle. Can you imagine constructing a large motorcycle from scratch that actually worked? He did it! The problem came when trying to get it licensed. It was made from such a conglomeration of parts of different brands of cycles. I think they finally decided it had more "Norton" parts so called it a 700cc Norton. Dan took me on rides. Furthermore, he taught me how to drive it. But the family finally put its collective foot down when I drove it into a 6 foot thick thorn fence where it stopped in the middle! I was held upright on all sides by the thorn bushes! I had forgotten how to turn or brake at the last moment! Dan didn't chide me. He only asked me if I would like to try again after he had extricated us from the thorns. What a sweet guy!

The revolution in East Africa when Tanganyika became Tanzania, while terrible in many ways, did our family the favor of allowing us to keep our children at home. We sent Esther home to the States to live with my parents for political as well as health reasons but we enjoyed the other three at home. I home-schooled Dan's Senior year. Beth and Joe attended the International School in Dar es Salaam where they were day scholars.

When we left Africa, Dan joined the Navy and saw service in Viet Nam. After his service ended he married and gave us two wonderful grandchildren, Lori and Ben.

They settled in Fairbanks, Alaska, where his adventurous life continued. He had a very demanding career and retired from ALCOM, (Alaska Communications). He had worked very hard and honorably at a job in which he was very proficient and in great demand. We were always so proud of him.

After Dan's divorce, he married Lynne, a lovely, competent, and compassionate lady. She is a Magistrate/Marriage Commissioner for Alaska. Together they have reached out to many people, pouring their lives and resources into helping others. Since his retirement, Dan, who is ever busy, has purchased a publishing company called Top Class and now puts out a very nice magazine in North Pole, Alaska.

Lori and Norbert married and settled in Fairbanks and have two grand little boys, David and Jonathan.

Ben married Rosie in New Zealand and with their son, Elijah, have moved to Alaska, as well.

Nearly two years after Sam's promotion to Heaven, I married Verne MacKinney, a family friend from church, and Dan's Scoutmaster from years before! We were married in Alaska by Lynne, in a lovely service where Dan gave me away, Lori was my Maid of Honor and Ben was Verne's Best Man. We were so happy and blessed and Dan and Lynne provided the most wonderful honeymoon for us as well! God bless them!

Ruth and Sam with Dan, at 9 months.

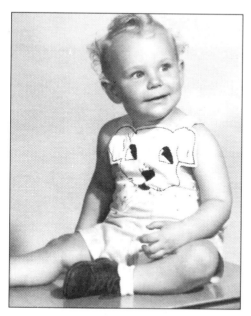

Danny, 1 year old.

Danny — 2 1/2 years old.

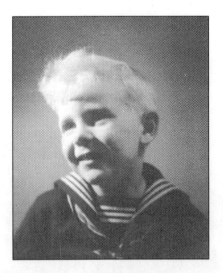

Danny — 3 1/2 y ears old.

Dan the hiker.

In East Africa Dan made a motorcycle from dozens of pieces from many brands. It worked well. Since it had mostly Norton parts it was licensed as a 700 CC Norton.

Dan in Alaska.

Dan and Lynne.

Dan with Alaskan Communications.

**Bright eyed Elijah doesn't miss a thing!
Dan's grandson**

— *Chapter 19* —

Esther Elise
Every Child Should Have a "Gramma" Like Esther

But....I am getting ahead of myself! She didn't start out being a grandmother. She was the smallest of our four children at eight and a half pounds, and was born on September 18, 1948. She joined fourteen months old Danny, and Mommy and Daddy at home. We were still living in the tiny trailer on campus at Central Bible College. Yes, it was small, but it was our first "home." We loved it, except that Sam's forehead managed to make contact with the door jam every time he came in or went out the door!

It was quite the day when Esther decided to be born! Actually, I was on my way to see Doc Johnson for my weekly checkup, when a taxi driver, in a great hurry, ran a red light and with a resounding crash, plowed straight into me on the driver's side! The police came and took down all the particulars. Danny wasn't hurt and neither was I, thanks to our merciful God! The police noted my condition and drove us to the doctor's office. It didn't take them long to determine the baby would soon put in an appearance.

I was in St. Johns Hospital where labor started and got stronger as the evening progressed. September 17th was my birthday and I was delighted my baby and

I were going to share our birthdays. Not so! She did not arrive until 12:01. I begged the recording nurse to put the date on the 17th as it would mean a lot to us as the years went by. I will never forget her gruff reply, "You wouldn't want me to lie, would you?"

The next day my Aunt Lillian Riggs brought me a clipping from the *News Leader*.

It was the accident reports and the birth reports. There, side by side, were stated, "Accident to Mrs. Ruth Beckdahl on Booneville Avenue," and "Baby girl born to Ruth and Sam Beckdahl at St. Johns." I kept the clipping for years, to prove we were celebrities making the news in two columns that day.

When Dan had been born he was completely bald, later developing white fuzz all over his head. When Esther was presented to me I gasped! Her head was covered with dark hair, even down the back of her neck! I had expected a repeat of Dan's hair style and was sure there was a mix-up of babies in the delivery room! They showed me the wrist bracelet, with "Baby Beckdahl" on it. I figured that even that could have been switched! I looked her all over and her toes convinced me! The second and third toes were joined like mine! She was indeed, "Baby Beckdahl," and how I hugged her!

She was mine, all right! In a week her dark hair started falling out until it was soon all gone and replaced by blonde fuzz! She was a pretty little girl and we had lots of company visit our little home to welcome our new offspring. She was a good baby, too.

We had a small canvas travel baby cot between our 3/4 bed and the wall. That was Esther's bed. Danny slept on one end of the couch. We were very cozy. We didn't have a bathroom so we hiked down the hill to the bath and laundry house. For Danny, we had a small potty under the bed.

Our heating system wasn't great either. An oil furnace by the front door often left the "bedroom" area cold. We put a small electric coil type heater in the 12 inch hall. When she was old enough to toddle around, Esther lost her balance once and backed into and sat on the heater. Her little "toosh" resembled a waffle and hurt her a lot, poor girl. We dispensed with that heater, it was a luxury we could not afford when it was so dangerous!

As soon as Esther could walk, she showed a propensity for mischief. Teasing Dan was her favorite sport. He knew he was not allowed to hit her so refrained. When our backs were turned she often would pull his shoe laces free. When Dan would yell and we looked around, she managed to be nowhere near him and would look up with an angelic smile as if to say, "Who? Me?"

Dan would look up with big tears filling his eyes and rolling down his cheeks trying to suppress a whimper. As he would point to her, she would grin and shake her head in a "I wouldn't do that" smile.

It happened frequently until I paddled her bottom. Then her mischief would take another form....hiding his spoon, or even one of his socks. Aunt Lill dubbed her "Ratsabella," a German expression meaning little mischief maker. Dan called her "Esther Pester"! Truly, she was a happy child, and always had to be busy.

Woodstock School needed a teacher and the Missions Department asked me to step in. So, two-and-a half-year-old Dan, fourteen-month-old Esther, and I left Springfield for India on the Mission Aircraft "Ambassador." Sam followed shortly when his classes were done at CBC.

When it came time for school, and we had to put the kids in boarding, Esther cheerfully accepted the reasons for it. She excelled in school, seeming to learn by osmosis. She enjoyed her friends at school and loved sports competition, art and reading, and history. Very early in her life she gave her heart to Jesus and sincerely wanted to follow Him.

During furloughs, Esther made lots of friends in school and church. She was active in choir and Youth Ministries, and in the drama, music, and art departments at school. For her Sophomore year we were asked to go to Tanganyika, East Africa to work with the large East Indian population in the city of Dar es Salaam. This meant new adjustments, new friendships, and a new boarding school, Rift Valley Academy, in Kijabe Kenya. It was a good year for her there in many respects, but her health had some big challenges. That, along with the political unrest that came to rock East Africa at the time, and the difficulty of some of our children's adjustments to the school, went towards our decision to take them out of RVA and keep them at home with us. The younger two were able to attend the International School in Dar es Salaam and the older two studied at home by correspondence.

That year was also good for Esther in other ways. We had some wonderful family time living so close to the ocean beaches, the incredible wild life available to us there, and some adventures because of the civil disturbances that were pretty scary for us all. Then malaria and heat stroke took a further toll on her physically and in February of the next year we decided to send her back to the States to live with my parents, and to complete her Senior year. The family all drove down to South Africa together where we put her on a flight back to the USA. Grandma and Grandpa Merian had recently retired from Missionary endeavor in India.

It is amazing how you can take a person out of a country but never the country out of that person. India and Africa with their languages and people are still a big part of her life these many years later.

Esther met Jonathan Philip Hughes at Central Bible College and they were married the next year. Jon became a minister, a church planter, and a building contractor. He was a hard working, fun loving, dedicated family man and servant of the Lord. They had four children, a beautiful family, Forrest, Byron, Fryth, and Nathan. All are in the Northwest, grown, and married, with families of their own. But Jon did not live long enough to see that. After twenty four years of marriage, two of which he struggled bravely with a terrible disease, primary amyloidosis, God called him to his heavenly Home. It is a joy to see him in his grown sons and daughter, in their voices, in their manner, and in their great sense of humor, and now in the grandchildren as well. Leah, Mitchell, Janae, and Jared are Forrest and Debbie's four. Byron and Jennifer have four girls, Brynn, Paige, Emma, and Avery. Fryth and Jim have Stuart and Sadie. Nathan and Sarah have Katelyn. What a wonderful bunch.

God did not forget Esther. John Eley came into her life and what a prince he is! He is the original "Gentle Giant," adored by the whole family, including me! Truly a man without guile. They were married in 1993 with all the family included in the ceremony. Verne and I thank God for John.

In spite of all the transitions Esther has undergone by constantly changing countries, schools, living quarters, churches, and friends, and through the difficult years of her husband's long illness and death she continued to grow and expand her many facets. She surprises me all the time, even now!

Her talent for art is unending, she loves to draw, paint, sew and quilt. Her perennial flower garden is a joy to behold. It is a large English cottage garden and is the source of the arrangements she makes weekly for her church. She takes on the tasks of weddings, the gorgeous tiered and decorated cakes and floral aspects as needed. She especially loves opportunities to lead and participate in Women's Seminars and as speaker at Retreats. God has used her understanding and wisdom in revealing Himself to hungry hearts.

Her kitchen is a haven to her grandchildren who eagerly visit often and where they "help" Gramma cook, making cakes and cookies and sometimes dinners to take home. Games are played at the table, stories are read, and sometimes they make things like greeting cards, or tiny pieces of cloth are sewn into quilts. Most of all, they all know they are all genuinely loved. Therefore, the title of this chapter!

Esther loves people young and old. I am glad to be included. She has been an enduring joy and encouragement to me, her Mom.... Well, after she outgrew the shoe lace pulling stage!

Esther at eight months

Esther – two years old

Esther, 3 years old.
Beth

Esther, 1 year old, ready to travel outside our 15 foot trailer home at CBC in 1949

The family, Sam, Dan, Esther and me in
Nowabganj Gonda (Misson Boys school) in 1951.

Esther and Beth sharing their dolls with Tharu maidens
who were fascinated with the eyes of the dolls closing and opening.

Esther — the bookworm.

High School Junior

Esther as Jonathan's bride.

Jon and Esther's family. Forest, Byran, Fryth and Nathan.

Jonathan and Esther.

Esther and Jon's grown up family.

Esther and John Eley.

Esther and Ruth on the wedding day.

Part of Esther's vast and beautiful garden.

Esther's daughter Fryth Elise, her husband
Jim Rasar and their two children Stuart and Sadie.

Making cookies at Grandma's house.

Esther's son Byron and Jennifer's 4th girl.

**Forest and Debbie's four children,
Leah 9, Jared 1, Mitchell 6 and Janae 3.**

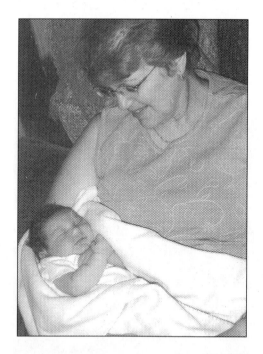

Esther holding 11th grandchild, Katelyn Beth.

Esther's daughter Fryth's and Jim's children in Lynden's tulip country — Stuart and Sadie Rasar.

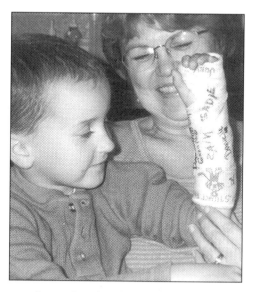

Stuey showing Grandma his cast.

Forest is a volunteer Fire Fighter in addition to his thriving building contractor business.

— Chapter 20 —

Elizabeth Anne
Beth —"Artist Extraordinaire"

After a long and difficult journey by train and a hair raising "lorry" ride up the treacherous hairpin turns of the mountain road, we finally reached the cooler atmosphere of Mussoorie. Our third child, Elizabeth Anne, was born the next day, May 13, 1953, very much to my relief! Dan and Esther came out of Boarding School and we were together as a family for a short time. It was good.

Up until the age of five, as was the case for most kids of that age, while up in the mountains, Beth got carried on the back of a coolie, in a basket called a "kundi." It was a long mountain mile to school, around the rocky, hilly and curvy paths used by the mountain people, mule teams, and donkeys, while monkeys bounded from tree to tree. It wasn't long before she walked or ran the distance to the school along with her siblings.

Beth's life has been full of episodes proving the guardian angels did double duty. Once when crawling around on the cement floor in the living room of our bungalow, she saw an intriguing creature under the cane chair. She grabbed it by the tail and brought it to me, saying, "Mommie—Makri" (Spider). What she held out to me was a very poisonous scorpion. Controlling my gasps, I placed my fingers over hers and pinched tight to prevent dropping it. "Let's take it out to the

"Borchikhana" (cook house) and put it in the fire." That is what we did. The burning coals dispatched him to scorpion heaven, if there is such a dreadful place! I sat down abruptly, shaking all over, and thanked God for His protection!

Another time when Beth developed a high fever, I put a thermometer into her mouth and said, "Now keep your lips closed." In obedience, she did, but she also chomped down on the thermometer and swallowed crushed glass and mercury! Although there was no medical help available where we were, God had said that He was a "very present help in time of trouble." I took Him at His word and called on Him to help us. Beth could have and would have died, but for God's intervention!

Through her lifetime she has had countless encounters with danger and death defying moments. As a teenager in the States, she was hit by a train while riding with some friends. They were dragged down the tracks and banged up badly but no one was killed. She learned early that it pays to trust God in all our ways, wherever we are!

Furlough times came bringing trials of procuring appropriate passport documents and visas. Because, I her mother, had not spent 10 years of my life in the USA, I could not pass on my citizenship to Beth who was born in India. Sam was not yet a US citizen. We had been in Bible College in Missouri when India gained its independence from Britain. Now there was no longer a "British India." So he became a man without a country for seven years and he and Beth had to travel on a lengthy "Stateless Document." After building up enough USA time, they were naturalized as American Citizens.

Different cultures and languages have always had

a large influence on Beth's life. Hindi, Urdu, and English were spoken interchangeably in our home. Attending boarding school in the Himalayan mountains during school semesters and living in tents along the borders of Nepal with us during winter vacations exposed the kids to many different life styles. Out in the "boonies" we became accustomed to the ways and delights of the jungle. We mingled with the tribes of Tharu people and the wild animals. Traveling by oxcart or elephant was not uncommon. By the time our next furlough arrived, Beth had absorbed much of the rural life of India on the Northern Border. Her sensitive spirit responded to life in any situation. This was good because our next assignment took us to Tanganyika, East Africa.

Once again the kids had to adjust to life in a boarding school. This time it was Rift Valley Academy in Kijabi, Kenya. Adapting to new people and a new language, (Swahili) wasn't hard. It was just something we accepted. But that year spent away from us was very difficult for Beth. Unbeknown to us at the time, she really struggled with feelings of abandonment. How we ached to undo that!

The term in East Africa brought new adventures and challenges. It was here that Beth first started her artistic expression. After seeing a detailed sketch she had made while sitting by me in our church service, while Sam was preaching about martyrs in the ring with lions, I was impressed to buy her some oil paints. Her first real painting was of a lion and Mt. Kilamamjaro done on masonite with oils. She won an art contest in Dar es Salaam!

After we returned to the States and Beth went on to High School. Versatility had marked her life. She had been in six schools in as many years! She loved and excelled in Art classes. She finally admitted to me that it grieved her that her art teacher paid no attention to her and gave her no pointers. This upset her so much that I thought it wise to go to Central High and inquire the reason for Beth being left to herself with no help. To my amazement the dear teacher replied that she herself was intimidated by Beth's tremendous talent and ability. She said, "I wish Beth would teach me!" Beth's fears melted and she enjoyed school more. She loved marching and choreographing for the "Kilties" Marching Band.

One joyous day Sam and I went to watch the crowning of the Homecoming Queen. Beth had been nominated one of the attendants. When she was declared the "Queen" and crowned, it was all I could do to keep from jumping out of the bleachers and yelling, "That's my girl!"

After graduation, at 17, Beth received scholarships for art and nurse's training. She entered nursing life and went on to study anesthesia. She married and then mothered three beautiful children. She ministered to many in the various churches where they served. She was gifted as an adult Sunday School teacher and did so much to add to the success of the wonderful Christmas pageants and musical productions.

Stephen and Nathan Shank, Beth's two sons are both in Seminary. Steve and his wife, Kara, have been ministering to young people in the Branson, Missouri area and will now be located in Texas. Nathan and Kari are in Seminary in North Carolina preparing for Missionary service in Nepal. He already spent two years there and Kari was in China at the same time! In Heaven, Great Great Grandma Elise Merian must truly be rejoicing to have her life long passion for missionary work being carried on through her line!

Beth's daughter, Christine Shank is a beautiful, lovely young lady. She is serving in the US Army and studying to be a doctor. She is a joy to be around and is a focused student at present and therefore doing incredibly well in her career. She is also in the Army of the King, as she loves and lives for her Savior.

Beth is a Registered Nurse Anesthetist. She puts people to sleep for a living! She works long, long hours and has recently taken a new position that involves a longer commute but the rewards of schedule make it well worth while.

She has the good fortune and gift from God to be married to Steve Gramith, a skilled rancher. Together they have built a beautiful home, designed by Beth, and have laid out their ranch in the rolling hills in Southwest Missouri. They raise registered full- blood Flechvieh Simmental cattle. Beth is owner and breeder of Foxtrotter horses. Beth and Steve graciously gave me a piece of their lovely ranch on which to place a doublewide manufactured home. Beth designed this house as well as her own and I sure do love it. We had it placed to overlook their beautiful ranch and its gorgeous cattle and horses. It also means that we can be together when Verne and I come back from church building projects. God has been so good to us!

Beth and I have gone back to India and Nepal several times. She took her son Stephen to visit Nathan who was in Nepal at the time. She so enjoys visits from her grown children. Her passion is still art and due to her diverse background, combined with her present rich life, the subject matter of her art is varied in medium and subject matter. She is an incredible potter, a painter of wild life, scenery and multi-cultural people. She wants always to reflect her love for the Creator and His creation.

Beth is highly skilled in too many areas to mention. She is very creative, an intense learner and worker and amazingly diversified. Anything she does, she does with total dedication and concentration, with wonderful results!

She is loved and appreciated totally.

Elizabeth Anne (Beth) arrived May 13th, 1953 in Nussooria, in the Himalayan Mountains in North India.

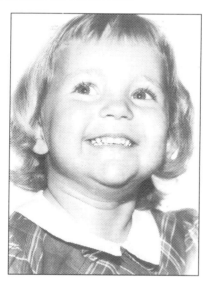

Beth's smile at 2 was contageous.

Beth ready for Easter.

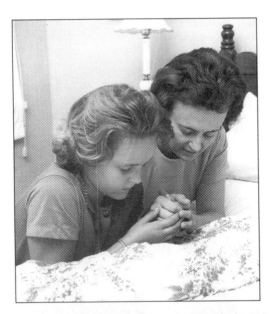

Ruth prayed with each child individually nightly while with us. So often they were away in boarding school.

Family "Story Time" was a much anticipated ritual.

During children's school vacation Sam made a little boat for them to play on the river, while Sam sat ready to shoot any crocodile wanting to taste a boy or girl.

Often Elephant rides in our compound or in camp provided fun for the children.

Our youngest children are carried to school in a "Kundi" around the mountain paths.

Beth is active in church and did many dramatic productions with her children when they were young.

Happy Wedding Day for Steve and Beth

Family fun in the snow with Stephan, Nathan and Christine.

Ride anyone?

Nathan and Kari's wedding.

Beth transformed a 15 ft. tall tree in their front yard by carving it into an eagle descending on its nest. She used a chain saw and chisels and a scaffold.

*The following is a small sample of Beth's artwork...
pottery — paintings of animals, birds,
people of all cultures —
in every medium*

— Chapter 21 —

"Up, Up and Away"
(Joe's Story)

This is one of the hardest things I have assigned myself to do: writing the story of my youngest son Joseph, his life and premature death. Joe played a special part in my life and walk with God.

Joe was born in Springfield, Missouri on one of our furloughs. It had been a difficult pregnancy and because of my illness I had to leave India and travel to the States without Sam as he was engaged in special meetings and would follow me shortly. Our three children and I boarded a ship stopping in London. While we were there, a general strike shut down our forward journey. After two weeks in a hotel God led the travel agent in locating someone's canceled flight plans leaving within the hour! It was already evening but I scurried around preparing the children for flying, something new for them. We had the use of two seats for the four of us at the front of the economy class cabin.

It was fun for the kids to be served "supper on a tray" soon after take-off. It was even fun for them to scrunch up and go to sleep on the floor. As soon as Beth was sleepy enough I got her curled up on the seat next to me. Dan and Esther played "Up, up, and away" with their hands making like airplanes. Gradually sleep overcame them and away they went to dreamland.

"Fear not, neither be afraid....I will be with thee, I

will help thee, and uphold thee with the right hand of my righteousness. I will never leave thee nor forsake thee."

I was so glad for God's promise of help. I missed my husband. I had to make all those plans by myself and care for the children while making split second decisions. Although Sam wasn't there, I was sure he was praying for us as he was conducting the meetings. I was so glad he would be coming, too, in a month. The missionary doctor had advised me to leave quickly while he could still clear me for travel! We had not anticipated the confusion caused by the shipping strike in London.

The night was EXTRA long and morning seemed like it would never come. We were flying WITH the time. Soon the children were slept out and hungry! It was hard for them to understand why I kept telling them to try to sleep and we would have breakfast LATER! We had boarded so rapidly I had no chance to prepare for this contingency and the flight attendant wasn't prepared for hungry kids! That was the longest "night" of my life!

After a plane change in Chicago we arrived in Springfield ready for some "DOWN" time! A friend came to the airport and whisked us away to Mission Village where a cottage had been prepared for us. It became "Home Sweet Home" for the next year. It was wonderful that the Mission Department made this provision for missionaries coming home on furlough. Sam arrived a month and a half later. Our baby was due in two weeks.

Two weeks passed and no baby. Two more weeks and labor started and stopped. Then it was really hard labor. The doctor said the baby was lying sideways and he tried to move him into position. NO GO! Hard labor continued and my Uncle Ralph Riggs and Aunt Lill came to the hospital. He called on the "God of Miracles" to turn the baby. No sooner had he said "Amen" when Joe turned over in correct position and was born in 10 minutes. What an answer to our prayer! And what a joy to see our bouncing baby, ten-and-a-half pound Joey!

A relieved Dr. Johnston got a big hug from Sam! We felt like we had been hugged by God! And we thanked Him and praised Him for His intervention. We were so grateful for my Aunt and Uncle and their prayer and loving care!

Joe never stopped growing. He was a happy, robust child and very loving. Eleven months later we were on our way back to India on a passenger freight ship when he took his first steps. The ship rolled and plunged in the angry waters of the Mediterranean Sea. It was truly comical to watch him trying to keep his balance! He never gave up and would laugh and try again. This same attitude was exhibited right through his short life of 30 years.

Joe had an incredible spirit of adventure. He loved to hike and hunt and camp with his older brother. The Himalayan mountains provided great vistas for exploration. He learned early to trust God and loved Bible stories. He absolutely believed God could do anything and often brought me up short by saying, "God already knew about this, Mom. Let's just ask Him!"

One day, when he was six and we were back in Springfield on furlough, I was called to the school for Joe. He had become sick with a high fever. He was listless and quiet as I put cold compresses on his forehead while he lay in bed. "Mama," he said, "I think God wants me to go to heaven to help Him get your house ready for when you go there."

My heart skipped a beat! Was he telling me something? Was the Lord going to take my little boy to heaven soon? I was so grateful when he recovered! He had had hepatitis.

Joe was all boy and he never lacked for friends. As he grew, so did his faith. He was full of life and adventure. He had already been throwing newspapers for two years in Jr. High and had saved enough money to buy a bicycle and his own clothes. At age 15 he wanted to go to work for Tiny's Steak House. He told them that they needed him as a cook! They laughed and said to wait until he was 16 and then to bring in his birth certificate and they would give him a job!

The day he turned 16, he took his birth certificate and presented himself at Tiny's and said, "Here I am, put me to work!" Strangely enough, they did, washing pots and pans! He worked hard and also observed the cooking angle. It was a natural for him. He soon recognized the regular customers and how they liked their steaks. As soon as he saw them come in the door he would put their steak on the grill and have it ready, to their liking, as they approached. He made quite an impression and a steady clientele. Within six months Joe was Assistant Manager. He saved his money and bought himself a red Camero and got his driver's license. He loved his car but he bought a motorcycle as well, "to save gas"! In his senior year at High School he was slated to be Valedictorian in spite of working 40-50 hours weekly at Tiny's!

One day after work he and his friend Matt went on a trip down to the Mark Twain National Forest. It is a beautiful area in the Ozark Mountains. They had planned all week for the adventure. It became dark and mist collected in the dips and valleys. The motorcycle light was unable to adequately penetrate the rolling mist and on one of those dark spots an escaped black Angus cow from a nearby farm was in the center of the road. The collision with Joe's helmet killed the cow and rendered him unconscious.

Matt, who had been on the pinion seat was thrown from the cycle but unhurt and he walked back a mile to the town they had just come through to call the Sheriff. An ambulance took Joe to the hospital in Springfield. They called us to give us the news.

We found Joe alive but unconscious. He remained that way for a week. God spared Joe's life but his concussion was so severe he could not function in school. He was such a determined kid that he tried and tried but couldn't retain a thing for more than a few minutes. The doctor explained that his brain was "coddled" and it would take months, if ever, to regain full use of his mental faculties. This was terrible news but Joe was very determined and he agreed to drop out of school for the rest of the school year and come back to finish the next year.

Joe said that he did not want to waste the time but wanted to go back to Africa to the Rift Valley Academy in Kijabi, Kenya where he had attended school when we were missionaries in Tanzania. There, he would ask to be allowed to make a football field for the school, which he knew they needed. He still had some insurance money from the accident, and he proceeded with our blessing.

We believed that God could bring about his healing. He honored His Word and did just that! Joe left by plane and went to a missionary we knew in Nairobi. They were kind and gave him a place to stay until he contacted the school where he accomplished what the school had wanted for a long time!

Many months later we met Joe at the airport. He looked fatter than when he left and it didn't take us long to find out why. He was wearing all his clothes so he didn't have to carry them! (3 sets of underwear, 3 pants, 3 shirts, 2 sweaters, 3 pairs of socks) He had had them on for three days!!! He was carrying two game trophies and a brief case. We wasted no time in getting him home and into the tub! He was rank! Phew! But best of all, our boy was well!

September came and he registered again for that senior year of school at Hillcrest. He had to work a little harder at learning but he wouldn't give up. He made it! Once again he was announced as Valedictorian and was also welcomed back at Tiny's!

Joe was happy. His adventurous soul wanted to see Alaska. They said there were no jobs up there. Joe declared he could find a job anywhere. A friend from church was going to Alaska. He asked if he could go along and would gladly pay the $100. requested to accompany him and he could also do half the driving. We prayed about it and Joe asked God to give him a sign if it was His will. While we were still standing in that circle the mail man came and Joe had to sign for a letter. It was from a friend he had helped out of a financial jam in Kansas. It contained a $100 bill and a thank you note. That is how it was for Joe. He always seemed to get answers from God. That week Joe went to Alaska, leaving his car, and a few of his belongings with us. Joe settled in Anchorage first, but later moved up to Fairbanks, where his brother Dan now lived.

Joe's heart was bigger than his body. He had a knack for finding people who needed help. He had no trouble finding work for he would do anything for anybody. The troopers in Alaska liked him because he would paint the jails. One day he called home and said, "Mom, I'm in jail." When I gasped, he laughed and quickly explained he was painting it not occupying it! He climbed 200 foot towers to install electronic equipment, when no one else would. He earned the nickname, Human Fly!

He wrote such loving letters of appreciation. Any little beautiful stone, or feather, or shell, he'd pop into an envelope and send it to me. He had climbed many mountains and would always send me the top most stone he could find. I have the top stones from Long's Peak in Colorado, the one from Mt. Kilamanjaro in Kenya, one from Australia and from New Zealand. His letters were fabulous journals of his adventures in places I have already mentioned and also in Europe.

Joe fell in love. He was betrayed by someone close to him. His heart was broken. His spirits spiraled downward and took comfort in a friend who tried to console him. He was caught on the rebound. She went to church with him until they were married and then quit. One mistake followed another. My heart was broken. Soon she was pregnant but their relationship had no future. We prayed desperately for them and that God would bring Joe back to Himself, clean him up, and take him "Home," if need be. God answered our prayers. He got back in church and serving the Lord. When their darling baby girl was born, he took her to church and presented her in dedication to God although her mother would not come with them. My heart ached and rejoiced as he carried Brandi up the aisle in his arms, asking God's guidance in his and his daughter's lives.

The difficulties at home did not diminish so Joe started divorce proceedings. They lived apart after the divorce but Brandi grew and adored her "Daddy Joe." He got to have her with him on the weekends. When she was four she was very bright and took a lovely picture of her daddy. It was the last one taken of him.

His friends in Australia invited him to come "Down Under" for his next vacation. An opportunity too good to be missed, he leaped at the chance, and off he went. He had been gone several months scouting business prospects in Australia and New Zealand and made some fine contacts and even commitments while there. When he returned, via Hawaii, he spent several days with my brother Bob and his wife Rose who were working with the USIA there. He phoned from their home, saying, "Mom, you will never believe how God has blessed and used me these last two months. I am so happy knowing I am in His will and loving care. There is too much to tell you by phone on Uncle Bob's nickel but I'll see you soon and tell you the whole thing. I love you so much." We said good bye.

He left Hawaii the next day and landed in Anchorage. There he had a few hours wait for his flight on to Fairbanks so he went to a picnic, his old company was having for their employees. Before getting on the back of his friend's motorcycle he had a discussion with David telling him that it isn't wise to ignore God's tugging on our hearts. It is important to make sure of God's forgiveness and His life changing Power as we never know when our lives can end quickly. They prayed together and started for the airport. He had moved to Fairbanks near Dan who was also now in Alaska.

A driver in a stolen truck, high on drugs, careened out of a parking lot and smashed into them, crushing Joe's skull but leaving David unhurt.

He was rushed to the hospital from where the doctor phoned us to say that Joe was alive but gravely injured and not expected to live. I phoned my cousin Merian who lived there in Anchorage asking her to rush over to the hospital to see Joe, which she kindly did. She got there just before Joe breathed his last breath and David stood by to tell her all Joe had said to him before getting on the motorcycle.

Merian phoned us to say that Joey would never have any more heartaches or pain as Jesus had just taken him "HOME." We fell on our knees and prayed and wept. "The Lord giveth and the Lord taketh away. Blessed be the name of the Lord."

Sam and I went to Fairbanks heavyhearted for Joe's funeral. The whole family was there. Motorola Company shut down for two days. They mourned Joe's passing for he was much loved at work. They all came to pay their respects. Many gave heartwarming testimonies of his friendship and kindness.

I have to tell you, in prayer I agonized and asked God where He had been when Joe was killed. The answer came as distinctly as if it had been spoken out loud. "The same place I was when My Son was killed!"

That somehow satisfied my heart. I was reminded of my earlier prayer, "Oh, Lord, bring him back to Yourself, clean him up, and take him Home, if needs be." Yes, God answers prayer, and He knows best.

Joe was now, "Up, Up, and Away." He remains so

dear to my heart and I know I'll be seeing him again someday, in Heaven with Jesus and all the loved ones and believers of all ages whose transgressions have been blotted out and have been given Everlasting Life.

Joe two days old with the family.

Joe grew up loving animals.

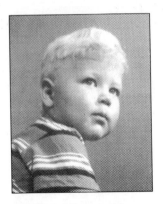

Joe – 1 year old

Joe entertaining a Tibetan Monk on our door steps.

My two lambs.

Joe — Always industrious.

Joe and Ruth outside railway station in Anchorage. July '79

Joe's adventures never ceased. His friends remarked, "He lived 60 years in his 30 years."

My son Joe's grave marker.

Joe's daughter, Brandi and I visiting Joe's grave the year after his death.

— Chapter 22 —

Samuel Thelle Beckdahl
"Home Is Where God Takes Us"

I've had many, many homes.....

Lakhimpur, Kheri, India, where I was born, and later served;

New York City, where Mom and Dad had their first furlough;

a cottage in Landour, Mussoorie, in the Himalayan Mountains, where we children and then our children spent four months of every year attending school, as day schoolers.

In Benares and Allahabad, in India, where we had a bungalow, while Sam served in the British Indian Army; Mission Village, in Springfield, where our family spent furlough time; Nawabganj, Gonda, India, where Sam was in charge of a Mission Boys School and Orphanage; In tents on the Northern border of India and Nepal; Several in Tanganyika, East Africa; Several more in the Springfield area, upon our return from the mission field.

A faculty house directly across the street from Central Bible College gate, where Sam taught for 20 years;

Our first "bought" home in the country where we suddenly realized that we actually completely unpacked our suitcases and put them away in the storage closet!!

Our youngest son was graduating from Hill Crest High School by then!

Sam was a professor and loved his time teaching. I, too, enjoyed my teaching career in Springfield Public Schools. Our home was the "Grand Central Station" for visiting missionaries and C.B.C. faculty get-togethers. It was wonderful. God was so good to us, blessing us with a multitude of friends, both faculty and students. We loved our church and especially the rich fellowship of our Challengers Sunday School Class.

Since we were both teachers, we had the joy of being able to travel during the summer months. The "Macedonian Call" pulled us back to India and Nepal over and over. Sam was able to teach short term courses in many of our Bible Schools and he held seminars for pastors. What joy that brought to us, as we returned to the places of our childhood as well as our missionary endeavors.

After 20 years at C.B.C. Sam "retired," as did I. We enjoyed our time together on the "farm" with our dog, "Lady."

It was difficult when we learned that Sam was ill with prostate cancer. He had always been so robust and healthy. God certainly was good to allow us to have 52 years of marriage, a wonderful full life of service, and four children that had grown up loving Him. As he grew weaker, we prayed together, laughed together, sang together, and reminisced together. Yes, we even mourned together.

Our children, and their spouses, my brother Bob, and his dear wife, Rose, came from all over the States to visit, comfort, and encourage us, as the day of Sam's "Home Going" approached. A hospice nurse told us that most patients linger until their spouse leaves the home for some reason, before they make their departure. I smiled at the observation, until I went out to the post office to mail a letter with my son-in-law, John. While Esther and Beth sat by their dad's bed, the angels came to escort Sam "Home."

Later, we recalled that lady's comment!

It was such a comfort to have my dear family surrounding me. We knew Sam would love his new home, with Jesus in this latest move. I am sure it was the happiest of his countless moves that he had made, and homes in which he had lived while serving Him here on earth.

Sam's funeral was more joyous than mournful. My brother, Bob, gave the eulogy so eloquently, referring to many of our adventures and experiences, bringing up wonderful memories. Dr. Charles Harris spoke of his life's work and enthusiastic teaching at C.B.C. Our colleague, Missionary Norm Correll, told of God's amazing leading and protection during those days of danger when the Revolution ravaged East Africa. Psalm 91 literally sustained us. My daughter, Esther, read a letter she had written to her father a few days before his death, and I have included it here. Beth spoke and then sang so sweetly. Our grandchildren recommitted their lives to accept the baton of missionary service and Christian living that he had passed on to them. We let Sam wear his Nepali hat, as a token of his devotion to the Nepali people he loved so dearly.

Here is what Esther read:

At Your House — Springfield, January 1997
My Dear Dad,
    While I write this, you are dying. I have come to help you and to be with Mama for a while. It seems a little backwards. It has been good to be here. I wouldn't have missed it for anything.
    I have been thinking about a lot of things, Daddy. As I see it, most people have some pretty ordinary fathers, doing pretty ordinary things. We don't! With you, life has always been a huge adventure. I have been proud of you since I was teeny. To me, you were so handsome and so strong. As I grew and went off to boarding school, I knew that you were doing important work that the Lord had called you to do. It didn't occur to me that we lived an extraordinary life. It was just the way it was.
    Our winter school breaks were the best! I can see it now, the family all headed out to camp near the villages where you would preach and show films. We were cramped into the jeep and the trailer, with the big tent and all of our supplies. The roads were horrid, and often washed away. We would cross swollen rivers on makeshift pontoon bridges or try to drive through the mud without getting stuck. Sometimes we'd make it and sometimes not! We rode elephants, or oxcarts, or tongas, or we hiked. We saw some of the most beautiful places on earth. We met wonderful people, formed close bonds with dear, lifelong friends, and were introduced to many, many cultures. Such a heritage! Thank you!
    Your love of nature and wild creatures has been passed on to all four of your children, and from us to our children, and to theirs! Your love of the Lord, as well.

We used to joke about not asking you to pray at dinnertime, because you would pray right around the world and back again...forgetting that the food was getting cold! How we are going to miss your prayers! Even now, when things are getting mixed up in your head about other stuff, when you pray, it is so beautiful, and so clear.

You have mellowed over the years, Dad. You used to be so fierce, so disciplined and controlled and determined to get things done. I like this softer you, more gentle and sentimental, relaxed and loving. You have been unique, in the true sense of the word. There is no one like you, you are one of a kind! No one has been as regimented as you, even to brushing your teeth at the same time every day, or having tea time at 4:00 o'clock, precisely! Who else can flit between six languages in the space of three sentences, or be so unswerving in their faith and dedication to furthering the Gospel? Who else has such a jolly laugh or twinkle in their eye? Who else can tell stories like you? Who else sings so loudly in church while making up their own words as they go along?

Thank you for loving me, supporting me through my life, for loving and accepting my husband.

O, Dad, I am going to miss you!

Your loving daughter,
Esther

Here is the Lord's prayer for you in Urdu.
He hamare Bap—
Tu jo Asman men hai
Terah Nam Pac mana jai.
Teri Badshahat Ave.
Teri marzi jaisa Asman

men puri hoti hain
Zameen men bhi puri ho.
Hamari roz ki roti
Ajh hamen de
Aur jis tara ham apne kasurwalon ko
muaf karte hain.
Tu amara kasuron ko muaf kur.
Hame ahzmaish men na parne de
Bulke burai se bachcha
Kyunke Badshahat, Kudrat,
aur jalal
Hamesha Terehi hai.
Ahmin…………

About a year after Sam's death I found it difficult to care for our large home in Springfield with the five acres of mowing and leaf gathering. I finally listened to sage advice. With the kids' help, we cleaned and sorted and packed up, sold it and moved to Beth and Steve's ranch in Neosho, Missouri. They were so good to allow me to put my double wide manufactured home on their place! It certainly became home quickly. It really wasn't hard to move or adjust as I had been doing that all my life. I loved the home immediately! I decorated the place and put up a large painting Joe had made for our house in Springfield, "Home Sweet Home." I was happy there and could honestly say, "Home was where God took me."

Ruth and Sam

Sam took great pleasure reading to his grandchildren, Lori and Ben (Dan's children)

Our first home after years on the mission field.

Wherever God took us, Sam and I loved to make a flower garden.

As Sam's "Home" going neared, the family enjoyed a time of fellowship. Only a few days later the angels escorted Sam to heaven.

Sam's grave.

Sam and Ruth

— Chapter 23 —

Verne Ballard MacKinney
"Verne, the Icing on My Cake"

Weeks and months passed quickly. I drove to Springfield, about 80 miles north to visit Central Assembly, specifically, our Challengers' Sunday School Class, the dear friends of 20 years.

While in the foyer, a friend from that class came over and gave me a welcoming hug. It was so nice to chat with him. About 6 months previously, Verne had lost his wife, Jean. She had an accident with an eighteen wheeler on the highway. Her little car was no match for the big rig. According to the State Trooper, she probably never knew what hit her, so quickly was she ushered into the presence of her Lord!

We chatted a while then I went into the Sunday School room where Sam and I and Verne and Jean had been attending for years. In fact, we usually sat in the same row! I found my usual seat was empty so gravitated happily to the spot, waving to old friends as I went! What a comfortable feeling! As soon as Verne had grabbed his cup of coffee and downed it, he came in. The only vacant seat left was where Sam had always sat, next to me. So, we smiled, again!

It was nice to be back with friends. I "came to" when asked to lead in prayer. I truly was happy to be there. After Sunday School and Church, my cup of joy was full, with lots to think about, and much for which to praise God.

The drive home to Neosho went quickly as I recalled all the friends and their news. It was a nice reminder of the past. I was especially grateful for the unique welcome Verne had given me. There was an unspoken bond established as we had both lost our spouses recently.

During the next week, I felt like calling Verne to express appreciation for his spontaneous welcome at church. He, too, seemed pleased at our "chance" meeting. I asked if he had been at the Credit Union Banquet four months previously. He hadn't been, and I told him that I had, and at the end of the banquet they had drawn the ticket stubs out of a hat for prizes. The very last one had been my ticket number! What fun! I had gathered my senses enough to go up and accept the two tickets to the Christian Comedian Show in Branson! I had brought them home and promptly forgot about them after depositing them in a bowl on my dresser. At the time, I had thought that I would much rather have won a pound of coffee or some sweet smelling candles! That very morning, my daughter Beth, had spotted my tickets, and reminded me that I had better use them. That is when I had thought of Verne, and thus the call to him.

I didn't know how to approach the subject, but finally got around to say, "Now, Verne, I don't mean anything by this....but would you come with me to Branson to use these tickets?"

His reply was, "Now, Ruth, I don't mean anything by this either, but... Yes, I'll be happy to come with you."

It was decided that I should find out the time and place and call him back. While I was doing that, Verne did a little sleuthing on his own, and when I called back, he asked, "Why don't you come to Springfield on the day of the show? We could have lunch together and then go to Branson."

He had found out that the IMAX theater in Branson was showing "Everest," on the same evening and wondered if I would like to see it also! I told him that I would love that, especially since that was the part of the world where I had been born and raised.

What a day!...First to Verne's in Springfield. Our lunch turned out to be a box of macaroni and cheese and a can of spinach eaten at the counter before we left for Branson. I love macaroni and spinach! We saw the comedian's show in the afternoon. Then we hit the ice cream parlor and felt like kids as Verne ordered us the tasty mint chocolate chip! Yummmm! Instead of walking around for a couple of hours waiting for the IMAX presentation, we decided to sit in the car and talk.

It was wonderful to feel so at ease on our first date. We talked and we listened. We learned that we were very much alike. Although we had been born half a world apart, our family upbringing was surprisingly similar. Our theology was the same. We had each lost a mate. We had even both lost a grown son. God had dealt with us in much the same ways. We both wanted to continue serving God actively. Verne was clear about needing someone who would be willing to go with him in the "RV" Church Building Ministry, traveling anywhere that God called him to work. That was precisely what I had spent my life doing! I had led a life of camping, and constant moving, as we served wherever the Lord led. It was not hard for me to picture myself in an "RV" role. In fact, I felt that I was already prepared for this very life, though I did not commit myself to it openly. I wanted nothing more than to know this was God's leading! But I did not want to jump in too quickly!

My children knew Verne even better than I did! Verne had been Dan's scout leader in the church troop. Esther knew him from singing in the choir with him every Sunday. She had commented that she had always liked him because he was friendly and kind to the young people. Joe had Jean MacKinney as his English teacher in Junior High School. Actually, Sam's and my contact with Jean and Verne was mainly in Sunday School where we enjoyed each other's remarks and comments on the lessons.

Experiencing "Everest" at the IMAX was thrilling and transported me back in time, but the main benefit of the evening was our feeling so comfortable with each other and learning that our hearts responded to the call and demands of the Master. In the weeks to come, we kept the mail busy with letters, and tied up the phone lines, too!

When Verne's birthday approached, I wanted to have a Birthday Celebration for him. I was tired of cooking for only one. So, I did it up right, with a big roast and potatoes, and vegetables and a birthday cake. He was very glad that I had not put coconut in the icing! It was fun to put all the remains of the dinner in plastic containers and send it with him as he was leaving for an RV assignment in Nappanee, Indiana, the next day. Later, he told me that he had enough food for four days from his birthday bash!!! We really enjoyed our evening together in my new Neosho home. Our hearts were happy, but we were also sad to think that he would be leaving the area so soon.

The days sped by and I was planning to go to

Fairbanks, Alaska in June to see Dan and Lynne. They were happy to hear of our budding romance. Lynne is a marriage commissioner in Alaska and suggested that we come up there, where she would be delighted to "Tie the Knot," Scripturally and legally! Verne and I had talked about getting married in our Sunday School class later in November. After coming home from Alaska, I was headed for Beloit, Wisconsin to attend our Woodstock School Reunion. That was not far from where Verne was helping to build a church in Indiana When the reunion was nearly over, Verne drove up and spent two days with us in Beloit where he met a lot of my class and school mates, who were in attendance.

I went back to Nappanee with him, where the Pastor's family kindly put me up. Verne would come in the morning to get me. I spent the days in his motor home fixing his meals while he went to build the church. We would have short visits for lunch but he would have to take me back in the evening. It was always hard to say goodbye and Verne and I agreed that this arrangement was "for the birds," and why shouldn't we go to Alaska and get married like Lynne had suggested! No sooner said, than planned and done! We were in our 70's and 80's and figured,.... why waste time?!

We got our tickets and went to the airport. There, I discovered our seats were at opposite ends of the economy class! I asked the ticket lady if she could get us closer together as we were getting married the next day in Alaska. She looked, punched a few buttons, grinned and said, "I can do better than that! Here are two first class tickets, on us. This is your first wedding gift!"

How sweet of the Lord to prompt such a kind response to our dilemma! August 6th was a happy wedding day. My grown granddaughter, Lori, was my bride's maid. Her brother, Ben, was best man. Dan, my son, gave me away. Verne and I sang, "Savior, Like a Shepherd Lead Us.".. Dan and Lynne gave us a royal celebration; a nice Church wedding, a beautiful reception, a honeymoon cottage on a river, and a Lincoln to "tool around in" in Fairbanks. Two days later they had all their friends over to have an August wedding anniversary dinner celebration for four couples in the group. The cake was cute with names on it. One couple "40 years," another couple, "8 years," next couple, "2 years," then our names, "2 days!" What a delightful time we had!

We left Fairbanks the next day, stopping in Seattle, en route, where Esther and her daughter, Fryth, met us for a short visit before we headed on to Memphis near where Verne's family was having their "Every 3rd Year Reunion." I landed there with 90 new and wonderful relatives! They took me to their hearts, and I love being a MacKinney. They are a close knit, happy family that God has marvelously led and used for His glory. Verne's grandparents and parents; my grandparents and parents, honored God and refused to raise children to populate hell. God has honored their commitment to Him. We are the recipients of God's promises and fulfillment.

Verne and I love the RV ministry. We love our little home on wheels, and have been living in it about 10 months a year for the last 5 years. I love Verne for his tenderness, and his consideration. He treats me like a queen. I love him when we talk about what is in our hearts, and when we don't need to talk at all! Our favorite song is ..."Oh Good Tidings of Comfort and Joy"!

We have comfort in each other, and joy beyond measure. We have the joy of the Lord in our hearts. I am the richest lady on earth having the love of Verne. He is now 84 years old and I am 80. We are still in the Volunteer Church Building Program, and we love it. As long as the Lord enables us we would like to continue church building. At the time of this writing, we are enroute to Massachusetts to renovate an old theater building bought by a congregation who wants it transformed into their place of worship... their new church! What a challenge!

I have been happy everywhere but surely, Verne is the icing on my cake! "HOME IS WHEREVER GOD TAKES US!"

Verne and I are happy in the RV Ministry of building churches.

Home is wherever God wants us.

In Washington State, I had Verne eating out of my hands. Raspberries — that is!

All the pieces must fit.

Verne (center) making sure the foundation is strong.

The walls must be strong.

A church goes up.

UNSWERVING FAITHFULNESS

Midst all life's fleeting changes,
The things which fade and fail;
The lights which once so gladdened
But now grow dim and pale;
It comforts and it heartens,
Whate'er may pass away,
To know that He is faithful;
To find that He doth stay.

Sometimes He has to test us
If He would faithful be;
And then His acts we challenge;
The end we do not see:
But He abideth faithful;
And so, throughout each test,
He heeds not our complainings,
But waits till we are blest.

So, through all lights and shadows,
Through all life's nights and days,
Through all its varied problems,
Through all its untried ways,
Unswerving, He'll be faithful,
Will fail not nor forsake,
Will guide and guard and keep us,
Till in Heaven's light we wake.

J. Danson Smith.

Books may be ordered from 6690 East Highway 86, Neosho, MO 64850-5204 or call 417-850-5319.

Or

From the publisher and distributor:

Cherokee Books
231 Meadow Ridge Parkway
Dover, DE 19904
302-734-8782

Books are $10.00 plus 3.00 shipping and handling